Walk

A Contemporary Guide to the Eightfold Path

VENERABLE HODEN

Copyright © 2017 Venerable Hoden

All rights reserved.

ISBN: 197460828X
ISBN-13: 978-1974608287

DEDICATION

To the awakening of all beings,

To the teachings that provide the way,

To the followers committed in doing so.

ACKNOWLEDGMENTS

I would like to thank the following people:

Dae Jih (Dr. George Sanders), who helped to prompt, support and edit this book. Also, thank you for your time and dedication to the DGZ sangha.

To my wife, Dae Seong (Nancy) for her unconditional support in my search over the years as well as the time and efforts to bring Dharma Gate Zen into being.

To all of those in the Dharma Gate Zen sangha, who spend their time and efforts to support the center and each other as we walk this path together.

CONTENTS

Introduction		1
Section 1	Balance	7
Section 2	Wisdom	25
Section 3	Conduct	63
Section 4	Mind	91
Section 5	Summary	117

INTRODUCTION

Like all internal journeys we may take, let's start with a question.

The question may be at the root of why you would buy or read a book about this path, or be interested in a subject that spans centuries. The question is simple, but the direction it creates may be complex, and the results profound.

That question is: *"Are you satisfied with your life at this very moment?"*

Not the satisfaction of "Do you have enough things in your life?" or "Do you think you have been successful?" or even "Do you feel alright?"

The question I just asked is the catalyst, usually, in why people start to look for answers. Many things in life may be good, or satisfying on a regular basis, but somewhere, in the back of their heads, there is something that doesn't seem right to them in their lives and in the world around them. I know it was for me. It was the reason I started to look around, start on a journey, a search to find answers to questions I wasn't sure how to ask.

I was not raised in religion, in the typical sense. We did go to a church for a short time, on occasion. I was aware of people around me that followed and believed in things, and I was like most people raised in the West, provided with an understanding of religion, and God, and different ways to view that word, "God."

But it didn't answer my question.

Even when I was successful in business, working for myself, collecting things, with a good house and car and marriage, I still had that itch in my mind. Something was out of balance. *There must be something more to all of this.*

You may also find yourself in this place, as many do. The idea that others may also be lost didn't provide comfort at the start, but eventually knowing I was not alone in this feeling did help me start to look around and see what others had maybe found in their lives and in their search.

What I discovered, after a long period of searching, researching, reading and exploring is that this is not a modern issue. It is a question that has been asked for a very, very long time.

Many found or created philosophies to help explain it, some through religion, some through science, this search for truth. For liberation. For understanding who we are and why we are here, and maybe more importantly what do we do with that information.

Eventually, I found an answer.

The answer however wasn't really an answer as much as a way to start asking the right questions, and a lifestyle that can help find a way to understanding these things. It was not found in the philosophy I read, or in the religions people practiced around me, or in psychology, or by just sitting around thinking about it.

This is where we should start. By understanding that the feeling you may have, and the answer you may seek isn't somewhere outside of you, it has always been within you. We just needed a way to find the right path to walk within ourselves to understand what is causing that feeling, our anger, disappointment, stress and lack of freedom. *We hold the key because we created the jail. It is just a matter of unlocking the right doors and learning to walk out.*

The Teacher

Many, many years ago, so long ago that it may be hard to imagine, a man was born, just like we all were born into the world. He also had questions, also didn't believe what he was taught about religion or society, and also started out on a journey to answer them.

This man was called Siddhartha, and we refer to him by his title the Buddha. He was flesh and blood, not a superhuman, just a traveler like you might be. He saw the world around him, questioned his existence and ultimately found an answer to what he was searching for: the root of suffering or dissatisfaction and an understanding of who we are and where we fit into this universe.

He was kind enough to share that information with those around him.

Not directly, as the answer doesn't help unless we are ready to ask the right question. He did however set out to give us a basic understanding of how to get there. He drew a map, so to say, a direction to follow for people so they can be ready when that question comes, to hear the answer, and more importantly how that can change our lives.

As he lived for many years after having his own awakening, he taught and spoke at length, in many areas, to many people. Many of these conversations were later collected and passed on through an oral transmission process over many years before they were even written down. They also changed as they were understood by many other awakened people over that time, developed upon and expanded. Each place this message traveled it was absorbed into the culture around it, and through that process each area developed their own unique version of this same basic message.

As we now find ourselves almost 2,600 years from the time he lived, the basis of what he said still has impact, even through all of the changes and development.

The Western world is currently undergoing that absorption of these teachings and many sources are available to us now, many more than were available to people in those centuries past. So it can be hard to extract what exactly he was talking about, since many of these teachings come to us not just through this vast time period, but also through the lens of other cultures that have been adapting and developing them much longer than we have.

When I started on this path in earnest, I was immediately lost. To even try to know where to start to sort through the multitude of versions of Buddhist thought, different schools, viewpoints, sutra (or stories), practice and history can become a part time job. Also to understand how to filter and extract the messages that fit within our modern world and lifestyle can be difficult at best.

However, I feel this was never his intent, for this to be an all or nothing path. Many people he encountered only heard a short message, a simple answer. Most of the teachings he gave were directed at those who had fully committed to the life of a renunciate, that is, a monk who has left his or her life behind to solely focus on this path.

Many of us will never do that, and that doesn't exclude us from this way of life. Even in the life you are in now, working, maybe married or single, maybe with children or not, no matter what your upbringing was, the color of your skin, male or female, whatever your sexual identity is, you can also find a way to break through your inner jail, break through your dissatisfaction and hopefully find a path that will lead you to your answer, when you are ready to ask the right question.

Untying the knot

Because the Dharma, the teachings of the Buddha, can be so vast and so complex, I have endeavored over the years to teach in such a way as to make them contemporary and approachable. I understand the draw for many to dive into all of it and become experts in the complexity and the scholarly pursuits behind the study, but in my view more knowledge won't necessarily make you feel better or lead a better life.

In my time acting as a monk, priest, or teacher among the people I have encountered, I find the majority to be like myself, back when I started. Busy people with jobs and responsibilities, in relationships, living in the world they grew up within, just trying to find a way to stop feeling like they are out of balance, over-stressed, and under-joyed.

The following sections of this book are a break out of three important aspect of Buddhism, and the first three things the Buddha ever taught: finding a point of balance in our lives, understanding where our suffering or dissatisfaction comes from and ultimately finding a way to understand and live better lives for ourselves and those around us.

This is a good place to start, as it is where he started. His teachings provide just this basis to get going, to start understanding and making changes in our lives. The application of this direction will vary, as we are all different, and we will have to apply this to our own lives for it to make a difference.

To that end, I have removed the language and terms that can make it more confusing, and have tried to make it approachable in our lives and the times we find ourselves. So it can be applicable here and now, and more than just a nice thought or academic pursuit, but instead a lifestyle and path I believe it was always intended to be.

Part 1: BALANCE

A man sat under a tree and declared to himself that he would not move until he resolved the root of suffering in the world. He would not have made it to this point if he had not first understood the importance of balance in our lives and thoughts.

This was the first thing that the man we know of as the Buddha taught and realized in his own training and life before waking up to the suffering that he sought to overcome. Balance in life, balance in thoughts, balance in actions. The path between extreme views or actions. It is the basis for the path some people walk in zen practice, how to stay equally balanced between sides.

This is called the middle path, and it can be achieved if we know how to find and maintain that balance point in our life.

If we can simplify the teachings of the Buddha to have a place to start, we can begin with this very first thing he taught, before the years and years he spent teaching other aspects of life and without all of the years of adaptation and cultural flavoring that has influenced Buddhism and Zen study.

To even begin seeking balance we must start off on a journey that leads within us, on a path of discovery about who we are, where we come from, what formed our opinions and direction in life. We must start to find the root of our suffering that has been causing us to feel imbalanced up to this point.

The idea of balance can be an easy concept to understand, the center point between two distant ends. We all probably grew up at some point on a playground and had the direct experience of this concept on a device called a "see-saw" or "teeter-totter." One child sits on one end, and one on the other and they take turns going up and down.

This is a close resemblance to how we live our lives, on one end or the other of the see-saw, going up and down in a continual motion, throughout our days. Sometimes we play both parts, running from one side to the other, and sometimes outside forces act as a counter-weight, pushing us up or pulling us down.

It is not easy to achieve a life of balance, at the center point of this device. It takes effort and discipline to change our motion from one end or the other to the middle. The center point is also hard to maintain once it has been found.

Maybe you have seen the gym equipment that looks like a round cylinder with a plank on top. The person puts a foot on both ends and tries to stay balanced and upright. The physical aspect of this is much harder, it takes strength and control to be able to do this, much harder than sitting on one end and pushing up and down. Even when we are in the middle we have to constantly adjust from one side to the other, to keep in the middle. Small forces of nature pull us slightly to and fro.

However, once we reach that balance point, it only takes small measures to stay there.

Getting to that point typically takes making great changes to our life.

This is where we begin on our path to change, finding a balance point between extreme sides in our thoughts, actions and behaviors.

This path we speak of starts with three very basic concepts; first finding a balance in your life, which leads us to understanding where dissatisfaction comes from and ultimately, following a structure of discipline to help us achieve a better, happier, more satisfied life.

However, without the first aspect, balance, the other two become hard if not impossible to accomplish.

Moving to the middle.

This balance is achieved through trying to reduce extreme actions on a moment to moment basis. Moderation is key. Small moves are needed to stay in the center. If we lean too far one way or the other, we are back on one end of the see-saw. Life will push us one way or the other constantly, so we need to understand how we respond to life, how our minds work, and how we can control those thoughts and actions to be able to make small moves and not extreme swings.

The idea of "balance" will be different for everyone, since everyone is leading their own lives. When people hear the idea of "balance" in their lives, many people say "That sounds good, I need balance!" Or maybe many people feel out of balance or feel something isn't right and so they search for a way to feel better and may find themselves in a meditation class, or a yoga class, or some form of religion. They may also look to outside substances or actions that will help make them feel better, without really getting to the reasons behind why they felt out of balance to begin with.

Balance becomes a strong word, a catalyst for understanding where our lives currently are, and a standard so that we can recognize what needs to change and to see for ourselves what side of the see-saw are we on.

In our lives, here in the western world, we are beset by extremes all the time, and sometimes even when we think something is really good, it is still not a balanced view.

We are also inundated by aspects of consumerism, in this richest of countries, which only seems to grow. Although we may not see it, it has a great impact on the balance of our lives and the balance of the lives of those around us.

When we bought our first house in Berkley, Michigan, we were shocked by the size of the bedroom closet. The house was built in 1927 and the bedroom closet was big enough to fit a broom or two and maybe a pair of shoes if they were stacked. This was probably more than sufficient space in 1927. People didn't have walk-in closets, nor did they own 200 shirts. Or 87 pairs of shoes. We have slowly started to build bigger and bigger spaces to have more room to keep more and more things. And when a new space becomes available, it feels "empty" and we search to fill the space with something more.

This extreme action has a lot of impact on us, as individuals and as a society, whether we see it that way or not. We of course spend more money now to live, to have bigger spaces, spend more on things to put in those spaces, many times with funds we don't have. We start to build a jail around us with all of those things.

This same action is also true in our minds. We constantly fill our open spaces with thoughts, emotions, memories and distractions that make our minds feel as cluttered as our living spaces. Our minds, like our living spaces become overstuffed closets.

When we follow this rush for more, it causes us to evaluate what we have compared to others, and what we don't have. Our things start to define us more than our character, and we work ourselves harder and harder to survive the financial outlay, and the upkeep to just keep our heads above water. And then we wonder why we are so stressed and unhappy. So we work more and more and we take less time off, just so we can afford more new things and keep up with everyone around us who are also acquiring more things, and our bodies and mental health can't take it, and so we feel out of balance. Our constant search for more things is like an arms race for our ego.

We also create an environmental impact - because all those things will not survive or last, and have to go somewhere. These actions are killing the balance of nature. If we can live more simply, remembering what we need, not what we want or think we need (or desire to get what everyone else seems to have). When we can live smaller, reduce our footprint, we can suddenly see that the cycle breaks and we find more balance. Our experiences of life over things becomes more valuable than the things we can buy. We also need less financial support to live, so we can stop working ourselves to death and start to be satisfied with what we have.

We are also living in an age of information overload. We are constantly being fed information and distraction through our attachment for more. Although some aspects of having information available is positive, much of it is not. We can be overloaded through negative information, misinformation, and subject to a not-so-subtle manipulation by those with an agenda to make us feel a certain way, buy a certain thing or follow a path that may not be healthy - physically or mentally.

We have become a society tied to constant alerts, distractions, and the need for more and more to make our life seem fulfilled and "tuned in."

We succumb to the alerts constantly ringing in our ears, looking down at our phones, attached to the feed of information to the point we become changed by all of the stories of actions of violence or anger in the world. It settles into our heads and germinates and creates anxiety and fear in our lives. It divides us, and contains us in our camps of what we think is true and right.

We create imbalance through these processes - because all things are connected, and every action has a reaction, a cause and effect.

The benefit from reducing our financial outlay, from breaking our habits of gathering more things and constantly watching mindless feeds of information leads us to being able to balance the use of our time. When we can remove ourselves from the merry-go-round (another device we used on the playground) of constant gathering and thing-buying and feed-watching, we reduce the amount of attention we have to give to maintain it, we find our time becomes a most valued thing. We also have more of it available to us, to spend in other pursuits that may bring us less stress and more happiness. Our lives end up having more value because we focus on filling it with life experiences we find value in, not with things that will never fill that space within you.

"But… I have no time."

There is a great zen saying: "Everyone should meditate for at least twenty minutes a day, and if you can't find twenty minutes, you should probably meditate for an hour, because something is seriously wrong with your life."

Trying to find time to balance our lives is a common complaint with almost everyone I know. There is never time to do what we want, because we have so much else to worry about (see above). Meanwhile, we are working ourselves to death.

It is beyond just imbalance, it is so extreme that it is shortening our lives. It's also like saying, *"I don't have time to take my medicine and get well because I am too busy being sick!"*

Finding time to find balance sounds harder than it really is. I know you may be thinking "I have to work that much, I have kids to support and look after, I have bills to pay, I have commitments, I have to keep up my house and accomplish a never ending list of tasks and errands. I have no choice". I used to say the same thing and that may be true of your life right now, but it isn't true that it has to be that way.

You can change these things.

My profession demanded that I spend every waking moment in work. Working towards impossible deadlines, creating, editing, meeting, talking, reworking and managing teams of people, who also were trying to do the same thing. It wasn't uncommon to work 60 to 70 hours a week, going weeks and even months where I did at least some level of work every single day. It wouldn't end, and I found a lot of pride in myself being the first to arrive and the last to leave. Putting in the hours was my badge of honor, taking on more than anyone else, moving up the ladder, getting more things as a result. But it didn't make me feel better.

Instead it exhausted me. It made me physically sick, mentally sick and depressed. It made me anxious, stressed, and unkind to those around me. I became a version of myself that was not an authentic version of who I was inside, being a person I didn't want to be. So through all of these actions and pressures and extreme ways, I was "living the dream" which in my case was actually a nightmare. I accomplished things I didn't care to accomplish and those actions had no lasting value. And I did it to myself.

So, I changed it. I changed how I live, what I chose to do, and what was of value to me.

Of all of those things you feel are holding you back, the truth is that the time you spend with your children will be more valuable than the things you give to them, and you will teach them in the process that being happy may just be better than having more stuff. Working all the time to make money to pay for things isn't as valuable as the wealth you gain from having time to pursue your passions, to have experiences, to take care of yourself.

"But… I still have no time."

We say we have no time, yet we spend an average of five hours a day on our smartphones. We also spend an average of five hours a day watching television shows. We are probably watching TV while on our smartphones, multitasking any number of things at any one time. We don't take a break from work because we can't afford to, or feel like we will be judged at our jobs. Yet this impacts our health and we are sick more often because our body is worn out and then end up missing work regardless, not to enjoy ourselves, but to recover.

So the time we think we don't have is actually being using to escape from the stress of the other time spent in stress and worry. We find time to offset our out of control life through escapism. The see-saw goes up, the see-saw goes down. From one side of extreme action and thought to the other. Day after day, until we either die, or wake up and put a stop to it.

This is why we need a way to live, to change our actions to allow our balance of mind. You can't expect to just sit in meditation a few minutes a day and find balance. It is not the solution to all that isn't working. It is a tool to help us to see where we need to adjust and change, so we can slowly move to the center.

Through meditation practice, we are turning down the volume on stress, anger and worry, watching our intent and our internal voice. We balance the negative ideation with clarity, with self-reflection. When we can balance our thoughts, control our impulses and focus on the middle way of the mind, we stop wanting things as much. We find joy in time spent in pursuit of passions not financial obligations. Our relationships change, our concentration changes and we see things differently. We have a chance to become more authentic to who we are.

Balance of the mind comes from deprogramming your habitual thoughts from the perceived truth and self generated dogma we grew up within. To stop and see the reality in front of us. The lives we lead, the actions we take, the direction it leads us. Without balance of mind, we are letting the dog walk us. It goes one way and the other, it pulls you off your feet when it sees a squirrel, it makes messes all over the neighborhood.

A balanced mind allows a balanced view. A balanced view allows us to manage our time. Balanced time allows us to break the cycle of things and information overload.

Once we understand how to see imbalance in our lives, and break the cycle of addiction for more extreme thoughts and actions, we can start to refocus our lives along a path that will help us to find that middle way.

"Ok, get to the path already."

One of the misconceptions I have heard a lot through the years is that our goal in this path or practice is to become a Buddha. It becomes an all or nothing pursuit, either absolute perfection, or this doesn't work at all.

Even the Buddha wasn't called the Buddha in his lifetime. He was simply a teacher. He strove to teach others not to become a Buddha, but to be more awake to the truth of ourselves and the world around us. The interconnectivity of all things. The truth of our existence and the conditions around that existence. To be an awakened person to these truths, a Bodhi (awakened) sattva (being).

This misunderstanding is also rooted in the often unstated question when people start this path, or come to our Buddhist zen center the first time, which is "What's in this for me?" or "What is the goal of this path?"

Sorry to tell you, if you are asking this as well, Buddhism offers no reward of heaven, no superpowers at the end of the road. It doesn't promise everlasting life, or even a never ending blissful state.

So our tendency is to question the validity of the doing of it, since we don't see a reward.

However, the lifestyle I am mentioning does have a goal and it is a powerful one. *Liberation.*

Liberation from suffering in our daily lives. Liberation from the veil of ignorance we live under. Liberation from the mental prison we have constructed for so many years.

This doesn't come easy, as we must wholeheartedly jump in with both feet to really find liberation from those things. Freedom is never easy, never a smooth road. It requires work and attention. It will need to be maintained as well.

When we remove the focus of becoming the next Buddha, and focus on liberation of self instead, we can place ourselves into an appropriate time and place. Just here. Just now. Just you.

The path we will discuss and break out in the following pages is not designed to make you a Buddhist, or more holy, or a monk for that matter. Its goal is create a better you, regardless of your background, country of origin, race, sexual preferences or political inclinations. To become a more awake person is a universal pursuit, and a self-contained pursuit.

The eightfold path, as the Buddha taught, is a process of changing the thoughts, actions and practice within us, to have a more rooted life. This liberation is the result of discipline of our thoughts, actions and practice.

Many times people ask why Zen culture is so structured, when we speak so often of liberation? We build a healthy structure around our lives, so we can grow better fruit, the same way a trellis is used in a vineyard to provide a foundation for better grapes. Grapes can grow without the structure, but they are more often less useful, less refined, less consistent.

This structure is self imposed for the most part, just you in your head with your thoughts, exploring the intent behind your actions. You must apply it inwardly to have an outward effect. Working with a teacher and being with a group of people also on this path helps, but it ultimately comes down to you.

It is also worth understanding that even though we speak of a "path" it isn't a road that leads you somewhere else. The eightfold path is a path within.

If you look at the universal symbol that represents Buddhism as a religion (below), you can see the elements of this path. It looks like a ship's wheel, with a center piece (usually with three commas chasing each other), followed by four bands. There are eight spokes, which is why it looks like a wheel. Often people describe this as "eight spokes leading out from the center." However, I see eight spokes leading into the center. Eight practices that converge through the four bands (the four truths) to the inner balance of self (through the three aspects of our lives: internal refinement, wisdom of the world and a community to practice within).

This path doesn't have an express lane. There is no monk in the world that can bring you immediately to balance. It is a path you follow into the self, moment by moment.

Even on his deathbed, the Buddha told his followers to pay attention to the teachings not the teacher. Find your own way to apply these ideas, this lifestyle. Don't follow blindly, learn from evidence you find yourself. Remove self-dogma and challenge the truth around you, even challenge what the Buddha said until you can see it for yourself.

"But…The Buddha lived 2,600 years ago, why would I care about this now?"

Why is it so important to follow a path into ourselves? Why should we care what went on 2,600 years ago, or hundreds of years ago in some mountain monastery with some monks? Why should we try? Isn't ignorance bliss after all?

The days we find ourselves in are rife with mental disease, lack of compassion, anger, judgmental views of race and sexual preference. We wage wars overseas and wage war against science and truth at home. We are nations filled with substance abuse, physical and mental abuse, depression and medication. We are literally eating ourselves to death through our diets, causing heart disease, stroke, diabetes, cancer and other diseases to skyrocket. Our stress is at an all-time high due to the last three decades of the changing demands of the workplace, financial pressures, and our consume-or-die lifestyle. Our planet is showing the signs of damage due to our insatiable appetite for energy consumption and waste.

Our lives as human beings are out of balance. Extreme action and lifestyles have been normalized. We are our biggest problem facing our future.

If, by some chance, we can start to take control of our lives and break the cycle of all of those things, the world will be a better place, now and in the future. Fixing you will help fix the world, because each of us is tied together, inextricably, even if we don't see it.

Every action we undertake in our lives has a reaction, positive or negative on the world and others around us. Those actions that happen around us have impact in our lives, and we have a choice to make. We can either perpetuate the negativity, or we can change the direction. World leaders, governments, religion or philosophy can't change the problem. Nor can they live your life for you. It is up to us to take control and live the life we want to see.

Through the last 2,600 years since the time of the Buddha, everyone who has ever lived through those times were unable to overcome issues like war, or poverty, or hatred. However, through this same time, many people who followed this path found liberation and relief amidst the same troubles we face today, and passed it on, from teacher to student, and those who listened also found balance, happiness and liberation.

Once we understand that we need balance, and that we are causing our imbalance through our choices, we can start to walk down this path into our core self and see the causes. When we find the causes, we can start to overcome them, and when we overcome them, we land in the middle of the see-saw, away from extreme ways.

Those who traveled this path through all these centuries and found liberation created wisdom around life, and this is the next element we will need to uncover along the way.

PART 2 WISDOM

The eightfold path, the advice the Buddha gave on how to live our lives, can seem confusing and difficult to understand, even when the explanations of each are relatively simple. They are like lamp posts along a road, but with no real directions on how to get there. Seeing a light in the distance doesn't necessarily mean the path to it is direct.

It is also often thought of as eight steps, since we are very accustomed to thinking this way in the West, like a five step program to lose weight, or the twelve steps in Alcoholics Anonymous.

The eightfold path doesn't really work this way, one at a time. It's a more holistic route that brings all aspects together at the same time to create the balanced life we have been outlining.

Instead of going through eight things to think about, breaking these into three concepts, which is actually how the path is categorized, may make it easier to understand and ultimately start to apply to your life.

The eight pathways are grouped under these terms: **Wisdom and Insight, Virtue or Discipline,** and **Meditation or Concentration** of Mind. This is how I intend to talk through them, as each section of this book covers each independently, but ultimately they are all part of the same path.

If we can focus on just these three aspects to integrate into our lives, we can apply a lot of different paths, many beyond just how we view the eight I will have outlined.

The Creation of Self Wisdom

The first one, **Wisdom or Insight** applies into our lives in the way we regard our experiences and how we learn from them.

Wisdom is experience and understanding combined. We can say that if we experience something in the world and have a good reaction, or a bad reaction, we learn from these experiences and behaviors and alter the way we think or regard the world around us.

As children we may put our hand on a hot stove even though our parents say to be careful, and so we get burned. We develop a sort of wisdom about that experience. "Stove wisdom," let's call it. It sounds like one thing, but it contains a lot in that one experience. We learn about heat, stoves, danger, pain, that some things can hurt us, that our parents are smarter than us, they watch out for us. Just one experience can teach us many different things and, if we truly understand those lessons, we can develop wisdom.

The same is true of ourselves and our self-reflection. If we can turn down the noise in our minds and then with a clear head examine ourselves, examine our behaviors and the results of those behaviors we can create "Self Wisdom" in the same way.

We may get to the root of how we see the world around us, how we interact with the world around us and the results of our actions. Then through "Self Wisdom", we start to see things that may or may not align with our current beliefs and we can also begin to see the motivations behind them.

For instance, we may be under the belief that we need things to make us happy. We need titles and a lot of money and new smartphones and cars and big homes, or the ideal of the perfect body to make us have value. But when we see the truth of those pursuits, like the additional stress it creates, how those things don't last, that we are being manipulated to buy more, that those things don't make us happy in the long run, we start to create wisdom around our lifestyle, impulses and habits, which allows us to change those things about ourselves. The wisdom gained through this changes our volition, our intent behind purchasing things, about our needs, about what makes us really happy.

So wisdom allows a combination of our experiences and understanding of self to live a different way. We have been doing this already, for a long time, to create the person we are now. We are, after all, a collective mind of our past experiences. They all come to bear at any point to define our personality.

If we act in an unkind manner all the time, or give in to impulses constantly, we draw from those collective experiences when we have an encounter. We use that experience to react in the moment. We draw from the only set of experiences we have, our past negative or positive reactions and we respond from that database of behavior. This is what starts to define our lives even as young children.

The creation of you (the condensed version).

We start early in life developing our sense organs, our eyes start to work, our ears develop, our touch and taste form. As this happens, our understanding of our physical form, and our interaction of that physical form within the world around us is created.

Our consciousness through these organs is created and collected, what something sounds like, what something tastes like. Our "stove-wisdom" gets stored along with everything else. From this we build our preference files.

I like chocolate, I don't like Brussels sprouts. I like music, I don't like the sound of an alarm. I don't like being burned by the stove, I like the feeling of a cool pillow at night. I like the smell of burning leaves, I don't like the smell of skunks.

We add modifiers to all of these as well, we may like milk-chocolate but not dark chocolate. We like the smell of burning leaves, but not wet burning leaves and so on.

I read an article that researchers at Cornell University found through study that we make 35,000 decisions a day, typically 200 on just food alone. These decisions we are making constantly are driven by our preferences and modifiers, one way over the other, 35,000 times on an average day.

When we develop further, and get older, we start the process of learning from what is around us, the dynamics of our life and family and through our education.

Our parents start with the easy stuff, the cow goes "moo," the dog goes "woof," the cat goes "meow." We start to know the order and categories of things even before the experience happens. I knew what a cow was and the sound it made before I ever personally encountered one. However, I didn't know what a field filled with cows smells like until I had that experience and gained more wisdom based on that new experience. My "cow-filled field" wisdom was then updated.

However, we also hold and retain a lot of knowledge about many things we never directly experience and rely on what we have been told is true. We accept others' versions of the truth, having no direct empirical evidence of those things ourselves, and those things also become part of our thoughts and conscious knowledge.

Over our lives, categorization starts to expand: what goes where, what is its name, how is it identified? How does the world operate? How does society work? What is good action and bad action? What hurts? What feels good? What is dangerous, what is safe? Basic functions to survive in the practical world. We build on them through our lives and they can change based on our experiences.

We may be open to relationships until we get hurt. We may live carefree until we face danger. Everything is always changing, always adding to our minds and our base for understanding the world around us.

Everyone you meet grew through this process in a different way. If you were raised in the Detroit area, you may view the changing seasons and adapt to the changing seasons in particular ways; if you were raised in southern California your environment would be different, the temperature, the surroundings, even aspects of language, would all be different than someone from Detroit. This creates a singular world view, based only on the information available as we grow. Even when we do experience new places and people, we judge them by our understanding of the world.

Religion can play a role at this point in young lives as well. Depending how you were raised, you may answer the question "What is God?" and "What is heaven?" in different ways if you grew up in a Christian family or a Muslim family. Or maybe you had none of these concepts in your upbringing, so your view is different and your answer would be different as well.

We are fed entertainment and stories that form our future life view from early on. Disney movies, and action films. We learn views on morality, and justice through books and lessons in school. We are taught ideas like "Happily ever after" and "The good guy always wins." We are presented with expectations of who we should be and how we should live our future lives, what jobs we should have, what path we should walk, how to be successful and make money. That we should find another person, marry, procreate, buy things, settle down.

It all gets stuffed into our craniums, in our gray matter, to be processed, tagged and categorized and it greatly affects how we live, think and regard the world around us. It sets our expectations as well. What we think should happen in our lives according to this plan set before us. However, most of the time it doesn't go exactly as planned and doesn't always follow what we were taught should happen.

We are self-created through these senses and our place within them, the world view around us, the culture around us, and we create our ego mind as we age, to act on what our preferences, expectations and basic desires call for: more good stuff, less bad stuff. More good feeling, less bad feeling.

The Result: Ego.

Our cumulative base that creates our ego acts out on these things constantly and seeks to find a place to fit into the world we find ourselves within. Our friends dress a certain way, we do it as well. We see people we admire in how they look or act and we wish to emulate them. People have things that seem important to them, so we want them too. The instinct we developed originally to just survive in our environment, find food, shelter and water has become a quest for things to make our ego feel good, to fit in, to feel safe, to not have bad things happen to us.

All of these choices come into play in every encounter we have in our daily lives. Our whole past combination of personality, action, reaction, result, preference and impulse, moment by moment in our lives. Our expectation of the world is created through all of these processes in our head and we use them to judge the current moment.

When we cling to our expectations and they don't match the outcome of our experience, we become unhappy. We suffer the results, even when they are close to what we wanted to have happened. We are so focused on getting what we want, something that fits our preference or viewpoint, that when something is even slightly off the mark, anger arises, or disappointment, or sadness and that is what we put back into the world. This also creates a loop of attachment, disappointment, future expectations, more attachment and ultimately, more suffering and dissatisfaction.

The Re-Creating of You.

So how do we undo this, or even attempt to change? I am sure you are thinking this all sounds daunting and impossible. But it isn't. You have always been in control of these processes, you just need to identify them, understand what is creating them and have the courage and effort to change them.

It will take time, as you may have to undo many of the things you believe to be true, or actions you have taken, or how you view the world. By building a new base, little by little you can undo the habits based on how you see, understand and react to the world, your life can be different and we can minimize attachment and the suffering that is created in doing so.

This practice combines two process: first to clear our minds through meditation so we can see into ourselves through self-reflection in order to understand how we think, how we act, and the reasons we do so. The second is to see the reality of the universe around us and how we fit into it.

From these two processes we start to move towards the middle between our extreme views and find the balance point of reality. Seeing the world and understanding what we see, so we can change our base of wisdom.

The Truth of the Universe! (The short version).

The first step in changing all of the aspects of mind we first need to know the truth of the natural movement of the universe and all that is contained within it.

You can read books, ask an astrophysicist, consult science, and study as much as you want. Due to the time you may or may not have to do all of that, the short version of this is to know and understand that nothing, I repeat, nothing stays in the same state. We, and everything around us, are in the process of moving somewhere else, changing into something new, every moment in time.

We can see this ourselves in the mirror, as we do not look like we did when we were six years old, yet we are still called by the same name. Our whole body has been dying and regenerating throughout our lives. We have been growing older, and physically changing our form each moment of our lives. Like a snake that sheds its outer skin, we are becoming different and new, all of the time. Constantly. Without end.

The whole universe moves, atoms vibrate, stars are born and die. The earth itself is spinning, but also moving through the universe as it expands. At any given moment the whole universe is different than it was before.

If we were able to take a snapshot of everything in the universe all at once, every person, every planet, every grain of sand and every atom in the universe and compare it to the same shot a day later, everything would be different. Everything.

All beings, all forms, even the dirt we stand on is undergoing change constantly. From the moment I write this, to the time you read this, everything is different in the universe. Every moment we exist is unique and will never be exactly the way it was, ever.

The direct experience of this truth can be hard to understand in the scope of our lives, since we see and experience things in very short moments. It's hard to see the gradual long term changes when we focus on the immediate present. But when we can pull back from ourselves and our lives, we can see the natural movement of all things in a constant state of becoming something else. If we could take those shots of the universe from day to day, it would be hard to argue what is true from one day to the next.

The impermanent nature of the universe includes us. We were in a different form before this form and we will be a different form after this form.

We can look at this nature of change in two ways, as a negative aspect or as a positive one.

The negative way is to not understand how things evolve and then cling to our desire for them to stay the same. This becomes very apparent in relationships, in career choices, in times of financial prosperity. When we are happy and satisfied, we feel like nothing can go wrong and we get comfortable with our position in that point of time. However, it is bound to evolve and change as all things do.

When this inevitable change takes place, we are stuck in the past version of the situation and do not adapt, and thus we create suffering and dissatisfaction within our lives.

Relationships change over time, because people change over time. They are influenced by the changing nature of the universe around them. As we age, our bodies change, our minds are different due to the collections of experiences. We learn new things, we replace the old things. Both people on either side of a relationship are going through this constantly. We often go through changes at different paces, grow in different directions and when that alignment starts to get far enough apart, the relationship breaks under the strain.

Our children grow up, our pets grow old, our homes change as things wear out, our locations may change even when we don't move. We don't look like, or feel like a teenager anymore as we age. Our hair turns grey (or falls out). We have less energy than we once had. We all become something different than we once were and we cling to that vision we have of ourselves when we formed that original self-ego of who "I" am.

All of this happens a little at a time, and if we are not prepared to change along with them, we become unhappy. This clinging or attachment is the root of a lot of our suffering, but it can be overcome.

We can also get stuck only wishing for the future or what is next, or some new place, day or time and miss the moment we are in. We are all "working for the weekend" or can't wait for that vacation, or retirement, or when we get older.

We can also worry when something is good that it won't last, and this attachment creates anxiety and stress, making the current good moment not quite as good. We cling harder to the great times in our life and want to escape from the bad times.

The positive way to view this change is that no matter what situation you are in, it will be different eventually. If you are suffering from a loss, or a downturn, a break-up, no matter what the situation, there is always a new version of you around the corner.

To know even in good times, we may have bad times again and gradually develop less attachment to situations to provide our view of good or bad. We move into the middle little by little and react less to the movement of the up and down of the see-saw. We can lessen our suffering by reducing our attachments to outcomes.

The inevitable change is something we can't stop or control, we can only control our understanding and attachment to it.

The Seven Billion "Yous."

Another important thing to understand about the world as it is and how it affects you, is that we are more connected to all things around us than we typically understand. All things that arise and change are connected to other things. This connection has a huge impact on our lives, yet we choose to believe we are at the center of everything. Our will is superior, and everyone is just living in our universe. We act like 7 billion little universes walking around on a planet bumping into each other. But this is not the truth of our existence.

The truth is that all things in the universe are connected and dependent on each other. The complexity is so vast, that it becomes hard to see and understand in the moment, in our place in space and time.

Even this ability to be alive on this planet right now, as you read this, necessitated a long, vast combination of events and actions that led us to this very moment.

The concept of the creation of the universe, the rapid inflation that started as a very small dense mass of heat and energy, and expanded at great speed and eventually cooled, over many, many millions of years, bumping into each other, cooling and forming, has an effect on you. You were there, in some way. What makes you now in this form at least was already there.

These events that were not in our control, events that we don't completely understand yet, were required for you to be here now.

The forming of this single planet out of so many worlds, to have the exact foundations for this type of life to be here, started a long time ago and developed over a very long period of time. The generations of life that lived and changed and died before we ever were close to being on the scene are responsible for you to be here now.

Once the form we are all in now as humans evolved, we still as a species had to adapt and roam. Multiply and hunt and feed. Survive in extreme climates, walk over mountain ranges and sail over seas. We moved to the far reaches of our planet over a 200,000 to 300,000 year time frame. Civilizations were formed, and destroyed, people moved and adapted and settled. Technology, from the first tool to the smartphones we use daily are a series of building and expanding knowledge from one generation to the next.

Blame your condition on your parents (and your parents' parents, all the way to the beginning).

We are bound by our ancestry, the generations upon generations that came before us, and survived. The chance meetings, the relationships, the lives they led, all leading up to who you are now in this time and place. Part of those people still live within you. We can see the traces of them in our genes and DNA. You have the body you have now because of them, and you are conditioned by what you have within that body, with this form. There are also many, many other forms that also have been doing the same thing over the same period, from the ant in your backyard to the atoms that comprise the chair you may be sitting in right now.

The things that create our form and make us in this shape, and have these functions, are the same building blocks as the stars. We are essentially made up of stardust and energy, and so is everything around us. And we are all moving together all at once into something else, all the time.

All of the living beings on this planet that have come and gone over long periods of time, all of them have an impact on who were are now. We can choose to ignore the symbiosis of all things and the dependence on the movement of the universe, we can hold fast on our view point and opinion, but it won't keep things from changing or what we truly are.

Change will come whether we want it to or not.

This long road of connectedness influences us all the time, how tied together we all are. Everything came from somewhere and everything is moving forward into someplace else, some other form, some other time, running into each other, sometimes over each other and dependent on each other.

"The efforts of those past and present…"

Consider when you eat a piece of bread, how many years back it took of collective adaptation and experimentation and expansion of our ancestors to make that single act possible. All of the development and understanding of agriculture and environment. The processes, the actions, the shared experiences and knowledge it took for them to adapt and change to their needs and environment over a long, long period of time.

Even if we move to the present, consider all of the time and labor that went into it; the people who work on farms, the energy needed through sunlight, the time it took for sunlight to be processed into energy for the plant to grow and change. It had to be nurtured, and protected and watered. It was then harvested, processed and packaged. Somebody drove that shipment to a place to be made into flour. It was mixed, and baked, and sliced, and bagged and boxed. It then went on another truck, or train to end up at a store. Someone had to unpack it, and put it on a shelf. One piece of bread took many, many people over time, through multiple efforts over centuries to make that just that one piece possible.

Now imagine how often you eat, how many things you own, throughout your entire life. How much effort was expended and technology developed, over centuries, for you to just survive the way you do? The web of who we are connected to, not just who we know, but the multitude of those we don't, all moving and depending on each other, all the time, is vast.

All actions have a reaction, and we are part of that flow, this inextricable net of connections create ripples around us and affect the universe.

Everything that happens around us also causes an internal aspect to arise, how we view, judge and react to what has arisen. Our idea of free will is conditional. It is influenced by the movement of everything around us and the impermanent nature of the universe. Internally we also have a conditional movement based on our thoughts and minds that are a collection of everything we have ever done. All of this comes to play at every moment of our lives.

This is the only place we can ever find a liberated will, in the choices we make based on the action we are presented with against the way we view the world around us. This is our intent and volition. How we create an action or have a reaction to what is presented to us in any moment. It is the only place to find freedom and liberation from our suffering and reduce it in others and in the world.

The ripples we make.

When we can understand the conditional nature of being at this time and place it should fundamentally change our view of the world around us.

It is a lot harder to be ungrateful when the crust is not cut off our bread when we consider how much went into the making of it, or to not waste the food to begin with. When we see everyone around us as part of the same family (and we are all from the same tribe when you go back far enough), it makes it harder to judge others or feel separate from them. When we do things that destroy our environment, we should first see how dependent we are on it to survive.

The ripples that affect us also form ripples we create along the way. What we put into the world goes off into directions we may never see. Our action and reaction, our causes and effects, influence the world we live in, just as all the other ripples affect us.

When we can pause, and understand with a clear mind what is arising within us when we get hit with that ripple, process it, understand it and control our response, we can influence the world around us in many ways.

This constant process of filtering ultimately creates a better mind, a better life, free from the attachment and suffering we create.

For example, when you are running late for work, you may become anxious. Everyone is in your way, the traffic is too slow, the construction on the road is causing slowdowns. The weather may be affecting your drive. You show up late, worried what your boss may think, maybe filled with resentment that you have to work at all, or that someone has power over you. You have bills to pay and things to buy and responsibilities and you need to have a job probably more than you want to. So you start to fill your mind with worry and negativity. You hold this feeling, and it starts to affect the interactions around you. When someone interacts with you, you respond with a mind filled with anxiety, worry, resentment and negativity. So a simple interaction has the impact at that moment of putting that ripple into the world.

You may take that out on a co-worker and say something unkind, or not give them your attention. That ripple now infects them, and they may feel upset or sidelined, or resentful. They take it to the next person or series of people. Now those people spread it to others, on an on, and even though your work day is done, and you are home, your ripples are spreading all over. Those people may go home feeling bad, or hating their job (or disliking you) and they create ripples at home, with their spouse or kids. On and on, over and over that ripple spreads. It no longer is directly connected to you, yet it has made a difference in multiple lives in areas we can't see or experience.

Our minds also start to fill in gaps from those types of experiences and create a narrative in our heads. Those people start to create an opinion of you, which creates judgment. They start to tell stories embellishing and creating various loops of "What should I have said?" or "Why do they always treat me like that? Is it me?" These bounce around in our minds and we spread that infection to the minds of others.

Just because we were late for work, which is a minor thing.

We can however change our ripples by changing how we deal with the situations that we are presented with. The phrase "the buck stops here" could be changed to be "the ripple ends with me" or the "the ripple was changed by me."

We can develop a mind free from worry and anger and judgement and not allow for things to affect us in such ways. We then can train our minds further to not allow these things to arise within us. Eventually as ripples wash over us, we change their direction into something different, something caring or kind. Compassion over anger, calm over anxiety.

This isn't just something we do in our heads, sometimes we have to change our lives to be able to do this.

If you are working long, hard hours in a job you are not happy with, maybe that needs to change. If you are in a relationship that causes anger or resentment, maybe that needs to change. You can't always think your way out of the issues, sometimes we need to change ourselves to be in a place to be happier or more content.

Many people I talk with have some form of this. They are in a situation that is causing them to feel unhappy, out of balance, angry, depressed, anxious, or unfulfilled. They feel trapped on top of it, because they have attached themselves to believing it's somewhere outside of them, outside of their control, causing these issues. They stay rooted where they are, waiting for something to make it better, never actually changing the situation they are in, or changing themselves.

As I stated earlier, this path is a way of life. It is not a way of thinking, or a magic pill, or a little bit of meditation to make it all go away. If we just convince ourselves to walk around in a state of forced happiness, we are just creating further delusion.

The understanding gained through looking at the nature of change and the abilities we can gain through changing our intent, allows us to understand the nature of ourselves. Who are we, what are we and where are we going? What are we putting into the world and what effect is that creating?

Unlike a Twinkie®, we have a limited shelf-life.

As we look at the history of where we are from, on this planet, and our place in time and space, we also need to dive into what we actually are and why we act the way we do.

When the Buddha was younger and struggling with understanding and believing the common religion in his time, he got stuck on an important aspect. What are we, and where are we going?

The common belief at the time was that there was a part of us, that was called Atman, a part of us that was connected to the cycle of living and was unchanging, or constant. In the modern sense, we may call this the concept of a soul.

This is a very important aspect for many religions still to this day. Something within us that continues on or goes somewhere when our form goes away. In some religions, that soul goes to a place, like heaven if we are worthy, or hell if we are unworthy. It may be reincarnated, or born again in another form, but still continuing, unchanged at its root.

However, as the Buddha saw it, this doesn't match the nature of the universe. All things change all the time, and nothing continues in an unchanging state.

So if there is no continuing self, then what are we and what happens to us?

The answer he provided is contained in understanding the combination of what makes us "us."

We are a combination of two things: physical form and mental formations.

We obviously have a form, but before we just pass that idea by, consider what we just went through and understand where that form came from, what it is comprised of: energy at it root, combined together, changing and moving, from the very same source as everything else in the universe. That doesn't make us aliens on this planet, it makes us, the stars, other worlds and aliens (if they are out there) all directly related.

Our form comes with conditions. It changes, it wears out, we are susceptible to sickness (just another invading form of life). We are in a certain shape so we can't just grow wings and fly, although some of our relatives do. We have hands and fingers and can do certain things. We need sources of energy and oxygen. We need to sleep, we process and export waste. We exhale byproducts. Our bodies are like walking science experiments, little factories taking in energy and exporting energy all the time.

Because we have a shelf-life, and will not be here forever, we have a condition of our health and safety. We self-preserve all the time, trying to get one more day. But our body is also somewhat fragile. It can break, it can get damaged. It can malform and grow things that can take down the entire operation.

This is something we don't like to hear, because it means the death of our "me." Our non-existence. Our non-being. And we are all mostly attached to life.

Where do we come up with these ideas of life and death? How do we understand the world around us? Where does that voice in our heads come from? Mental formations.

The Narrator in our heads.

There are four mental formations that occur in all of us: sensations, perceptions, impressions and consciousness. They have no form, no reality, no way to exist outside of our heads. We may be able to write down our thoughts, as I am doing now, but they are still not real any more than a photo of a piece of bread will satisfy your hunger. They only can create a ripple in someone else's mental formations when they are read, and processed and applied to what our view of the world currently happens to be.

The way our minds work is important to understand (using the minds we have to understand them) so we can actually see where our ripples are formed.

Our form provides input through our senses. We have eyes, ears, noses, tongues, skin, all designed to filter the world around us. We developed these abilities through the generations before us of creatures that survived environments with the aid of these abilities and moved on. Little by little over millions of years.

These abilities we have allow us to see and hear things. To touch and have feedback, to taste and smell. All of these processes that bring information into us are just providing data.

When you look at a bunch of flowers on a table you may be able to distinguish what color they are. You may be able to know what kind they are. You can see details of what they are comprised of. You may even be able to smell them if you are close. You can tell if they are real, or if they are fake.

All of those processes are just data. Your eyes do not see flowers, they only reflect light, which separates color. Your nose doesn't smell flowers, it only processes the tiny particles coming from the form of the flowers. All of these processes are taking place in your mind. Your mind sees flowers, your mind smells flowers. Your mind is what is making the determination.

This is how our mind works in a broad sense. It takes input from our surroundings and filters them into our understanding of the world around us.

Our consciousness is created through these experiences. We know our distance and our place in time and space due to the inputs we have through our eyes, our ears our sense of form (through touch), our sense of taste. Our conscious self is a collection of inputs.

Through our experiences over our lives we encounter things and learn things. We learn what other people call something (like flowers). We start to encounter flowers in our lives and we know how to categorize them, based on what we were taught. A flower is a certain thing, it looks a certain way. It smells a certain way. It feels a certain way.
As we get older and we experience more flowers, we expand that understanding. Some things may look like a flower, but we call them

weeds (even though they are flowers). We know that a rose is different than a daisy. We may start to break out the differences of flowers and how they are categorized, we may run into something new and think it is a flower until we learn otherwise.

This categorization happens with everything around us and is the nature of living in the world. It allows us to know what is good for us, what is bad for us, how we should interact with something. Pet a cat, don't pet a tiger (they are both cats). Put your feet up on an ottoman, not the coffee table (they both hold our feet up).

We can perceive things around us, filter that data into our minds and put them into a proper place.

It is fair to say that we have never experienced anything outside of our minds. Anything we experience, or can remember, or feel about anything is always inside our heads, filtered through these senses that provide data to respond to.

We like what we think, we think what we like.

Once we have all of these things and experiences in their proper place, we also apply a label to them based on our experiences inside our minds. We like something, we don't like something, we are neutral. These preferences that we attach to the things we experience drive a lot of our waking hours. We are always trying to get more of what we like and less of what we don't like. If we encounter something we are neutral about, we don't really care.

We may like roses, and not like daisies. We may like onions in our food, or we may not. Or we may like green onions, sometimes. It is a constant flow everyday trying to balance our "what we want" moment to moment, trying to feed our need for "like", and avoid "don't like." "Don't like" makes us uncomfortable and unhappy. "Like" makes us comfortable and satisfied.

This can also be influenced based on where you grew up and who raised you (parents, friends, society).

When I was young, my version of a "hot dog" was the hot dog that came from a street vendor in New York City, with bright yellow mustard, hot sauerkraut, and semi-soggy steamed buns. That experience of having a "hot dog" that way set a condition for me, and I now compare that hot dog to every other hot dog experience. I like them that way, and although I may have had various forms of hot dogs since that time, even with the same ingredients, I am still trying to replicate that New York City street vendor hot dog to this day.

I also make judgements based on what I consider to be a hot dog experience. When someone puts ketchup on a hot dog, I shudder. Even one element outside of my view of the ideal hot dog creates a response that rises within me, and I judge the item in front of me (and the person a little bit as well).

Now, consider all of the people in the world and all of the food they eat and what is common experiences for them, compared to yours and it's easy to understand how we create a database in our heads based on "right" and "wrong" ways to eat. It is not uncommon to see things like shrimp flavored potato crisps in Japan, or eat deep fried balls of octopus. What I normally view as a hot dog street vendor, in Japan they are in fact a grilled squid on a stick vendor (which are also delicious by the way, but it's no New York City hot dog).

Our preference of one thing over the other drives our volition, our intent and our actions as these all arise based on our collective experiences, of who we are, where we are from and how we view the world.

So we have an opportunity when a ripple comes to us to decide and react. When someone offers you food, we process what it is (if we can), we perceive the food, we categorize it as food and we move down the chain to see if our experiences match the "like" or "don't like" system of judgement. A hot dog equals a specific experience for me, and even if it's close, I still have issues that arise against my pre-conceived wants and needs.

If someone offers you pizza, we know it is pizza because we have had pizza before. We look at the pizza to judge what it looks like and what is on it. If it has mushrooms (we like those) but also has onions (we don't like those). It may be square, when I prefer round pizza cut into triangles. We filter what is in front of us instantly and we make a judgement and that creates an action. We may find a way to do both, by taking the pizza, but pulling the onions off to make it closer to our expectations. Or we may just pass altogether. Rarely, do we just accept what is provided as is, despite our preferences and just eat it.

This preference creates an attachment to outcomes we expect to happen, and we judge the outcome based on what we wanted our preference to be, even when it is an approximation of what you wanted.

This is why when a child in a restaurant orders "mac and cheese" and a gourmet version comes out, which may be a much different version than the glowing orange box version they get at home, they get upset. Their category of "mac and cheese" has been conditioned by the experience they have had in the past, and they have an attachment to what they want and like. The kind they eat, not something else that is also "mac and cheese" but looks and tastes different. Even when it's close, we still get upset.

All of these things combine at the point of experience and our mental formations start to arise, and we have our next action before us. Do we refuse it, do we cry about it, get upset? Do we get mad because our parents didn't give us what we want? What ripples do we chose in those moments to send into the world?

This is our intent behind our actions, the place where our inner voice lives. It creates situations, it judges and it determines what we do next. Do we send sadness out, do we send out gratitude? Is it close to what we wanted, or better yet, does it matter?

We can choose what we want to put back into the world, not just react on impulse like we are used to. In doing so, we can greatly alter the outcome of our actions.

Even monkeys fall out of trees.

Now sometimes, even with the best intent, our actions may have a result that was not good. We can't always make the best intention come into play. We have all tried to do something kind and it didn't go as planned. Handed something to someone, misjudged the distance and timing and dropped it before they could grab it. Held a door open for someone, lost our grip and let the door close before they could get through. We can have an intent to do no harm to our surroundings, yet still step on an ant. We can have the best intention, but we can't get too attached to the intended outcome. Our best chance is all we have.

When actions go less than anticipated, ripples still go out in the world from our actions. When we keep our intent in check, and try to do no harm, we create less situations for harm to occur. We still make the world and our minds a better place to the best of our abilities. Moving to a mind of compassionate intention we will more often than not, make a positive change to our surroundings. We will do better most of the time. We may even be able to laugh in the moments it doesn't work out as planned.

If we walk down the street, head held high and see an ant on the ground we have a choice. We can through good intent, be careful and step carefully. Or we can jump on the ant and kill it. The first way is good intent, the ant has every right to be alive like you are and just because it was in your way is not an excuse to take its life. This may sound small, but it changes our mind a little bit each time.

We may also walk down the street and not seeing the ant, step on it and kill it, even if we are being careful. Our intent stays intact, to do no harm. Now, the ant died anyway, but our volition was not to kill. Little by little, our minds in this way are changed as well.

The flow, the drop, the flow.

So the combination of our form, and our mental formations are what "we" are. There is nothing beyond the construction of our "self." As I mentioned a while back, the continuing-self is not a part of those five things, aggregated together to create what we think of as "me." Since our mental formations are not form, and our ego is not a form, and everything is changing and moving all the time, there is nothing of self to move on.

This leaves one aspect to consider, and it is a big question most of us ask at some point in our lives. So where do we go, if nothing of self moves on? The real question people are asking is "Why should we care what world we create if I won't be around to see it?"

Because we are part of, and have always been part of the universe, continually changing from form to form, as energy moves through time and space.

The energy that forms you moves into something else eventually. It doesn't look like you, and your mental formations are no longer part of the process, but we are constantly forming, un-forming and reforming.

This may be easier to explain through the following analogy.

In Shunryu Suzuki's book *Zen Mind, Beginners Mind,* he speaks about viewing a waterfall at Yosemite National Park and reflects on how like human life this is.

When I considered this concept it helped me to expand on that idea and maybe explain how this process of connectivity, where we come from, how we progress, and ultimately, where are we going. It is the closest I have been able to put into words how you might view and understand life, death and transition.

In some Buddhist circles, life and death aren't seen as concrete things or events but rather ongoing transformations that reflect constant change. To begin, it may help to visualize a mountain top, with a huge river flowing forward. The water in the river fills all the spaces around it, and it is bound by the natural forces that act upon it, like the gravity that pulls it down and forward.

Eventually, along the way, the river comes to a precipice, an edge of the mountain. The water encounters this edge and because of the conditions of the rocks around the edge, the shape of the edge, the force pulling it over, it starts to fall and break and separate.

This separation creates water droplets which begin to fall. The droplet is no longer attached to the river, it is now separate from it, still made of its essence, but apart from its source of where it came from.

At some point along the fall, the droplet starts to gain awareness of its surroundings, now that is is no longer part of the river. This creates consciousness of its place in time and space. It has a certain shape. Because it is contained in its shape, it can also see other drops around it, also separated into their own shapes. Each shape is a little different than the droplet, and it can discern the differences. Some look round, some look long, some are wider than others, some are small and some are very large, compared to the droplet.

It is also being pulled by the same forces of nature that caused the waterfall to happen, the wind may pull it one way, closer to the river, sometimes farther away. Gravity is pulling it along as it falls.

It can't remember being the river any longer, it only feels its own edges, its containment. It changes shape as it falls, ever so slightly, but it still feels like the same droplet the whole time.
As it falls it interacts with other things - maybe mud or rocks, debris that is also around the droplet, falling and changing as well. These

influences can make the droplet cloudy or muddy. It makes choices on what it allows in and what it pushes out. It may bump into other droplets and take on a part of them, either cloudy or clean and bright.

At some point, the journey to the bottom of the fall is completed, it lands back into the river and becomes part of it again, without shape. It can no longer remember being the droplet, because now it is the river again. It has no shape any longer.

Maybe there is another precipice down the line, and it can happen again, maybe the next fall is shorter, maybe longer, but the drop that forms the next time is not the same drop from before, it is part of the same source, but not exactly the same drop.

If you want to understand this let a drop of water fall into a glass of water and then try to pull the drop back out. Whatever comes back out is now impossible to discern from the water it went into. It has gone back into formlessness and shapelessness. It is no longer the same drop, but it is part of the whole again.

Here is why it matters what we do in our lives. If the droplet, along the fall purifies itself from the influences around it, if it pushes the mud out, the rocks, it becomes clear again and when it ends its journey, it adds a clean source back to the river. If not, it makes the river a little less pure, a little stained. That mud gets brought into the next drop when the next fall arrives. So the actions of each drop can have an effect on those around it, it can pollute drops it encounters, or it can become clean and pure. It is a constant flow back and forth from the same source, and each drop effects the nature of the river over and over and over.

(Spoiler alert) We are like the droplet in this story.

The river represents the universal source of energy we have all been formed from and the universal consciousness of all sources always coming back and breaking out again.

We may break from the source and have shape for a time until we return once again. Always changing, always moving.

The other drops we see are all the other forms around us, all the other people, animals, living beings. The forms of energy that create and define our world and elements within it. Everything is from the same source, they just look different. Some look like us, some look like ants, some look like elephants. They are all individual parts of the river, all headed to the same place, from the same place, all being pulled along through time and space by the forces of nature around them.

If we have influences that make us muddy, filled with rocks, cloudy in nature, this is like the ripples we put into the world, and what we bring back. We either make the river muddy or clean during our journey. It's our choice which way to go. Many people think only of this one life and one fall and create nothing but mud. Others work to balance out the river, to refine and create a better source to go back to and come from again.

So we don't have life and death, exactly. We are only ever part of the river, separated from the river, back to the river. What we were will become separated again, only changing shape, only a different form from the other form, over and over.

Self-Wisdom.

Now that we have gone through the truth of the nature of the universe, of our minds and our construction, how we process cause and effect, and the ripples we provide, where we are from, and where are we going, we can create "self-wisdom." The truth of who and what we are and how we interact with the world around us.

The next step is diving into how we create a framework to develop these aspects into real, applicable change in our lives. The trellis to grow our liberation from, and the tools needed to build it.

The understanding of all things we covered above won't matter if it is held intellectually without action. This is a way of living and doing.

To be able to change your intent, watch what arises within you, within your mind, and what you put into the world, we must have a system in place to overcome those impulses and make better choices, for ourselves and others. A framework to make our droplets cleaner so we help clean up the river within this lifetime and use every opportunity we have in front of us.

SECTION 3: CONDUCT

One of the key areas that helps to change our lives for the better is being in control of our desires, impulses and actions. By building a framework that helps us to make better decisions in the moment they arise, we create the space needed to deliberate and reflect on our options.

Typically, we are not aware of our moment by moment actions. We respond instantaneously without thought, and our choices are being made by our desire in that moment to fulfill a result without thought of our outcomes.

We can see this easily even if we track just one day of how our mind moves, acts and reacts to situations around us.

For example, if someone cuts us off in traffic, we can instantly react to avoid a collision, but at the same time a whole realm of feelings and thoughts arise within us. We then respond as each of these thoughts and emotions flood our minds. Our ego flares up, anger heats up ("That person almost hit me!"), judgement of the person and situation and their intent comes into play ("That person did this on purpose!"), fear shocks our body as adrenaline rises as a result of our fight or flight response, and all at once we respond. The response typically is to use your car horn for much longer than is needed, maybe shout something they can't hear, or in some cases provide a visual response to that person through vigorous hand gesturing.

However, the truth may just be they didn't see you. Or they were swerving because some other action caused them to have a response. It is entirely possible that all the things we think are true are true, that this was an aggressive move intended to hit you and cause you harm, but the chances of that are very, very small.

The much larger chance is it had nothing to do with you in any way, just being at the wrong place at that time when it occurred.

In that moment, we can simply avoid the situation, and let it go. Err on the side of it being unintentional, and then none of those thoughts and emotions arise. Control the impulse overload and quiet the mind before our response comes out.

If we track our decisions for every interaction and our responses to them for just one day, we would fill books with notes. It happens constantly in our lives, and the training it takes to be in control of our minds takes work.

Our minds control us much more than we control our minds. Our base desires, our impulses for food, sleep, sex, control and wanting things, drives our minds most of our days, even though we are unaware of them. So to become more in control we must build a framework of discipline on a regular basis that makes us pause, understand the situation and what is arising, and understand it before we react to it. It allows us the opportunity to check our intent prior to putting more waves out into the world.

In the process of watching what we do and how we react, we can start reconfiguring all of the tendencies toward just reacting, the same way someone who goes to a gym, little by little builds strength through working out. It provides a new version of our past responses and allows less noise in our heads at each encounter.

Walking down the middle of the road.

The most basic of this thought process and structure is the middle path, a balance between extremes, in all things. When we can understand how extreme our judgement can be in any situation, we can lessen that and find a happy medium between our actions, thoughts and responses.

This is the target for a lot of our disciplined structure, the balance point in what we do, and how we act.

There is a stereotype of the "typical Buddhist," one who is passive in all things, who never gets upset, who never does anything wrong. It has been reinforced by Hollywood and is the punchline of comics and jokes.

The reality of anyone, Buddhist or non-Buddhist alike, is that we all have thoughts and emotions and we can't stop thinking or stop having emotions. The lifestyle we are talking about is the dedicated control of our thoughts and emotions which allows us to have better outcomes.

I have been a monk for many years now, and have been practicing these techniques for even longer, and I still do have anger. It arises at different points for different reasons. I used to hold anger in for a long time until it built up and then I would blow up. Even now, when something makes me angry, I feel the same things arise, the blood pressure goes up, adrenaline rises, my mind often goes into fight mode.

The difference is now as those do arise, they don't get very far. I have become much more patient over my years of practice, I let way more things go. My ego isn't bruised so easily. I open myself up to let the pressure escape and it doesn't stay with me for days or weeks. I still struggle with some long term resentment, as we all do. Things from our past that still set us off, a situation, a person that has done us wrong. I actively work on these things that are no longer real (after all, they are completely in the past and in my head) and untangle them over time. As the knots get loose, they don't elicit the same emotions in me when I chose to let them invade my thoughts. Little by little I let them go so I can move forward.

The mind and memory itself is a fascinating thing. It can recall situations, usually not in as great detail as we think, and in doing so recreate the same emotional response as when it happened, in the current moment.

Our minds also add judgement and embellish the situation over time. Each time we recall something that makes us upset, we add a layer of new upset feelings over the last one. Like those candies I used to love as a kid, "jawbreakers," that consisted of a soft center, but layered over and over with a hard coating. We add layers of coating to our past each time we bring these feelings into the present when the core is usually something not as severe or hard as the outer shell. Also, like those candies, the outer layers get so large, they are hard to crack and hard to ignore.

When we build a structure around how we think, and what we allow to invade and take over, we can stop the cycle of living in the past and reliving things that upset us in the now.

We can also stop adding to the layers.

In some ways the control of anger, resentment, judgement and suffering is a war of attrition. We remove those things that we carry with us for years and years through practice and we also stop piling more on in the present. It is a lot easier to live a balanced life when we clean out the old and stop replacing old issues with new issues. Slowly, when we get rid of more than we bring in, we start to clear more space for better thoughts, less suffering and less judgement.

Following a middle path of how we regard situations, judgement and views go a long way toward achieving this.

Moderating our thoughts leads to a more moderated response. It even allows us to change our choice from one of anger to one of caring or compassion. From suffering to joy in our lives.

The choice has always been ours to make, we are just out of practice or were never taught how to create the space needed to make better choices. Our experience has led us to do it differently most of our lives, so it takes time to undo those actions and replace our former attitudes and actions with things that are positive.

The trellis we grow our actions upon.

The structure that we follow is based on guidelines that we create for ourselves to help us to judge a situation and provide us with a recommended path to follow. There are many versions of these guidelines, and monks typically follow hundreds of formal paths depending on the lineage they are with. Many of these guidelines were created way back at the beginning at the time of the Buddha and were just rules of conduct, to allow people in the community of followers to coexist in peace.

However, these guidelines are not just for monks and nuns. The most basic structure consists of five areas to follow and be aware of in our lives, at the time of decision and action, to give a structure to choose from. It helps us, like the trellis that grows vines, build a better course of action and help our intent in situations.

If we were to boil down all of the guidelines and things to think about, it comes down to this: *avoid doing harm to yourself and others in the world, and watch your intent behind your actions.* That's it. Two simple concepts that we can follow, if we have taken formal vows or are just trying to change our lives for the better, Buddhist or not.

If we can apply those two concepts to our lives, we would be much happier and so would the world around us. However, at any time or place, anything we encounter, any situation, it is not so easy to think of these concepts and how we should apply them to our behavior. It is also important to know that most people you encounter are not trying to follow these directions and are stuck in impulse mode, acting out their own internal issues and we are part of that experience when we encounter them. We can't expect everyone around us to be ready to do as we do, and so navigating our lives is something we have to work on for ourselves.

So we can start to follow five basic guidelines when we start the path that encompass these two ideas and provide to ourselves a daily reminder to make better choices in these areas.

Anyone can follow these, it doesn't require anything special. In the Buddhist tradition many people take these five as "formal vows" in front of a monk and the group of followers at their temple or center as a public acknowledgement that they too are trying to follow the same path as others.

The five basic guidelines are:

> 1. To not willingly take away life from living creatures and in doing so respect that all life is part of us, not separate.

2. To avoid actions, thoughts or behaviors that are mindless in nature.
3. To not take things that are not willingly given, or earned.
4. To be aware of our sexual desires, to not act impulsively and avoid doing harm in relationships with others.
5. To be mindful of our speech to others, promote positive speech and avoid negative speech.

In each case, these stand to help us make decisions in the most basic elements of our lives and provide a framework to build our lives around.

Because Buddhism is non-theistic, meaning there is no "higher-power" to look towards, we have nobody to be responsible to other than ourselves and our community around us. There is no heaven or hell to go to by following or not following these vows, simply that our lives will be better by implementing them into our thoughts and actions.

In some cases they may even conflict with each other in the moment and we have to decide which is the best course of action.

I use this question when we are talking with people planning to take these as formal vows: "If you are walking through a forest and see a deer pass by, and a moment later a group of hunters comes up and asks you 'Which way did that deer go?' what do you say?"

This creates a loop in the guidelines we just discussed, because if you tell the truth, which follows the guideline on using positive speech (avoiding lying is one aspect of that) the deer will potentially be killed. However if we follow the guidelines on speech, this action would then break the first guideline, to not willingly kill (or be an accessory to the killing) of the deer. So we have a choice to make.

Everyone answers this question differently (ask yourself how you would answer). There is no right or wrong answer, only your choice, your life, in the moment. You could also just stand there and not say anything which is also a choice, to avoid doing either. You could bark and run in circles probably scaring the deer farther away (and maybe even the hunters!). The answers are many, and in the moment you are provided with basic guidelines to act in a positive manner, but the application, choice and best outcome are still for you to decide. We ultimately don't know how each situation will unfold, and we have to be aware of snap judgements. So each of these guidelines we follow create a framework only, and we need to bring our best judgement to bear in the moment.

When we break each of these out in detail, we can see how many things are overlaid on each. They are not as black and white as they initially appear, and understanding each helps to see how our choices create ripples in the world, seen and unseen, and where our intent is created.

First: Respect all life.

With the first guideline we say to "not willingly kill but to respect all life." Many people believe this is a required vow of being vegetarian in our diet. But most of the Buddhist world is not, and even many monks will have meat in moderation. The Buddha was not a vegetarian, and didn't require the monks to be either. He only said not to knowingly allow killing to take place for the monk or nun to eat. So if someone was invited to dinner and they found out an animal would be killed for them for that meal, they would ask to spare the life of the animal. When people are begging for food, as monks have historically done, they take what is provided with immense gratitude, for the gift and the sacrifice that went into providing that meal. The word used to describe a monk in the Sangha is Bhikkhu (male form, Bhikkuni is the female form). The literal translation means "beggar" or someone who lives by alms (handouts). As they went around with a bowl in hand, asking for food, they accepted what was given with gratitude, and as the saying goes Bhikkhus can't be choosers (chooshus?). So if someone put a piece of meat in their bowl, they ate it with respect for the gift they were provided and they were grateful of the sacrifice made so they could survive yet another day.

The truth is even if we only eat vegetables, life has been take in order to provide us with a meal. There is a wide ecosystem involved in every meal, and if we respect ALL life, plants are a part of that. People will say they are not sentient, so it doesn't matter, but our vow is for all living things. Many insects are killed to protect those tomatoes so you can eat them somewhere down the line. Many animals are killed by the trucks driving those vegetables to market. We can't be self-justified in any aspect of our involvement no matter our diet choices. We can however have respect and gratitude for every piece of food we consume, because at some point some sacrifice was made to provide it. Choosing to reduce your intake of some forms of food, like meat, adding moderation to your diet and not wasting food are all great paths to follow, but we should have gratitude at every opportunity for what was provided to us so we can survive yet another day.

This also goes beyond just the food we eat. Insects are also alive, and you may not like them, but they are just surviving like you are. Just because a spider ended up in your shower this morning doesn't mean it needs to die for the intrusion. It is trying to live just as you are, and as we covered in the last section, you are more related than not, (so consider helping them out instead of bashing them with a loofa!).

I used to spend summer days wrangling ants out of our kitchen by putting them in a glass and releasing them outside. One or two is manageable, 200 at a time was becoming a part time job. My wife eventually found a bug vacuum that gently pulls them into a tube so I can release them en masse. It seems like such a small thing, a bug, a mouse, a fly, but all are part of you and part of life, and we should see them as such. Treat them all with kindness and respect for the lives they lead.

It should go without saying, but the same is true of human beings, and the judgements we make. Causing harm to others, or not caring what happens to the lives of people far in the future should matter to us. Leaving no trace of our existence, no harm to the environment (we need it to live), and treating all people with respect, regardless of how they look, or what their life choices are. You are just one life among trillions on this planet. So many lives will end on the day you are reading this, and many will come into existence. It is a constant process of form and no form, and we are not the only beings that matter.

Second: Mindless behavior.

This next guideline, avoiding mindless behavior is also a wide subject. It is typically reduced to avoiding alcohol and drugs, but that doesn't really cover all mindless behavior in modern times. Alcohol and drugs are a fast path to mindlessness for sure, but so are a number of other things. Having alcohol in moderation isn't as damaging as mindlessly engaging in other actions, such as all the time we spend tied to our electronics, our smartphones, and our constant information feed. Seeking constant pleasure in eating whatever we want, doing whatever we want, our need of consumption or for escapism, and not being aware of the impact on others around us are just as strong. Typically if people have a drink with dinner, or when out with friends, it is a short period, a set time. Mindless behavior in these other aspects tends to go on through our every waking hour. We fill our minds with things to distract us, keep us from feeling connected, and much of it influences our mind to become more judgmental, angry, or just motivated to buy more things. This starts to spill over into the world around us spreading this anger and judgement. Mindless behavior is many times at the root of our anxiety and suffering in the modern world, and it is increasing exponentially.

Being mindful in thought is not easy when there are so many distractions around us. It is good practice to be aware of how often our minds try and move us away from stillness, or being completely in the moment we are in. This is how our brains work, always scanning, always feeding back information. This is how our ancestors were able to survive in the wild all those years.

Many times we are seeking constant distraction because we are uncomfortable with the quiet mind. We start to see ourselves and the world around us, and we can't wait to get back to our comfortable world of not being present.

This becomes very evident when you remove yourself from the world for a short period of time on something like a retreat. If you have ever taken part in a silent retreat, just not being able to talk about everything at every moment to others can be enough to throw us over the edge into an uncomfortable state. Having no access to entertainment can amplify that feeling. Now add the inability to go to bed when you want, wake up when you want, eat when and what you want, and see how your mind reacts.

When I was doing my training in Korea, in a monastery in the mountains, with little to none of the comforts of home, it wasn't the culture shock that was hard at first, it was the complete lack of control I had on giving in to my mindless pursuits. There was no entertainment, no place for my mind to escape. I slept on a wood floor with just one blanket, we ate the same meal three times a day. We woke up at 3:30 am and went to bed at 10:00 pm. I slept next to other trainee monks, all in a row, 85 or so in the same room. Our whole day was a routine we didn't control. After a few days, I found myself settling in, and being away from the constant distraction feed my mind started to just be present. I didn't have to worry about where I had to go, I didn't think about what I was missing. Just there, just then. I became present with my mind, and the noise was at an all time low.

You may never have that opportunity, to remove yourself in such a way, but you can reduce mindless behavior in how you live your daily life, just a little at a time, until you find a balance between your mind and actions and learn to be mindful of what you are doing and what you are thinking. Watching what behavior we engage in throughout our day may reveal many mindless actions and impulses we act out on without a moment's hesitation.

Third: Take only what is freely given.

The guideline to only take what is freely given is also beyond the basic concept of not stealing things. Most people learn this when they are very young, to not take something that isn't yours. However, we do take things that are sometimes not freely given, such as time from someone because we can. We take advantage of someone, ask of them to do something for us as part of a barter system. An "I did this for you, now you do this for me" type of situation. By watching our desires and intentions, we can start to see this in our own minds. What is freely coming to us and what are we actively seeking to gain?

There is a travel joke about going to Japan that I learned and experienced while I was there. The joke is that you could leave your wallet on a park bench and come back a day later and it would still be there. Japan has been raised as a Buddhist society for centuries, and this is part of the culture, to not take something that isn't yours. It is dishonorable to do so. They also have an extremely high conviction rate (over 99%, which is debated, but that is what is reported). I have heard that this is because when someone commits a crime in Japan, they expect to be caught, knowing that they have done something wrong.

I also asked my translator one time how safe the area of Tokyo I was in while I was working there. He told me you could walk through the street with a 100,000 yen note (about $1,000) stuck to your forehead and nobody would bother you. I didn't try this, but I never felt unsafe while I was there, walking through the alleyways and streets of one of the largest cities on the planet.

Compared to the Western world, we have a very different reality. I see stories often of someone who returns a wallet, or a lost item and is regarded in heroic terms for doing so.

When I was in my late teens I was working on a job site in downtown Detroit. The crew I was on asked me to go pick up lunch down the street from where we were. While I was walking there I witnessed a man gunning down another man across the street in broad daylight. I didn't really process it at first, as everyone stopped and looked at what was going on, but I carried on with my task. I later found out that it was a waiter who worked at that restaurant who'd found out that the bartender stole his tips the night before. So he'd confronted him that day and ended up shooting him to death over what was probably only a few dollars. It was something that didn't affect me much at the time, but has stayed with me ever since.

I feel we have a long way to go to understand this vow in our society and the actions we take in response. How we view what is rightfully ours and how we defend that ideal, and who gets hurt as a result.

One way to practice this guideline is to try and give with no expectation of anything in return. To help without thought of "you owe me one." To give to someone in need without thought of how people might regard you as a good person. If you can let go of thinking about what you might get in return, you may find that you have less desire to want something, or even need things not freely given.

Four: Awareness of sexual desire.

The guideline about sexual desire is commonly referred to as "not engaging in sexual misconduct." This covers the most obvious aspects of sexual abuse and rape. But it also covers how we control our sexual desires related to our motivations and intent, which many times is hard to classify as "misconduct" in our Western view.

When we engage with our sexual desires we have to be aware that two aspects are in play. The first is the understanding of your intent behind these actions and the second includes the effects these actions can have on yourself and others.

It is natural to have sexual urges, and this guideline doesn't mean a required vow of celibacy. However our intent behind fulfilling these urges can bring situations into play that can cause harm to yourself and others. Such strong natural desires can lead to mindless actions and cause irrevocable harm.

If you are in a relationship with someone, you know that infidelity causes a great deal of harm to the person you are with and potentially the person you are with outside the relationship. Using sex as a tool to get something from someone else, manipulating someone through a sexual relationship, or judging others based on their sex (or sexual preference) is bad intent and should be watched and regarded as unskillful and harmful. Following the intent of our actions in this area helps to see why we are taking these actions and understanding that even if you feel something is positive, the other person may not. The pervasiveness of sexuality in our society can also fill our minds, and lead to a variety of mindless behaviors.

We live in a sexually charged world in the west, through the shows we see, the advertising we regard, the language and judgement of other people. It may seem like an easy one to maintain, but watching how the mind draws our attention to things we find desirable, we can follow back to our intent in doing so and make a better choice.

Fifth: Positive speech.

I saved this fifth guideline until the end for a reason. All of the other four are things that we typically go out of our way to watch, as choices arise, but this last one seems to be one of the hardest for people to implement, believe it or not.

The power our speech holds is not often considered in daily interactions and it is a primary source for most people to communicate. Our speech includes more than the spoken word, it includes any form of communication between ourselves and others.

We have all been in a situation where someone has said something that made us feel bad, or like less of a person, or conscious of our self-image or was in some way demeaning. A lot of those interactions stay with us for a very long time. Sometimes we even hold onto something that was said to us as a child all the way into adulthood. It's a direct way to influence someone's ego or mind. Consider the things that roll around your head at night, the situations we create, the stories we tell ourselves. Think of the issues you carry with you from your past, the times you questioned yourself, felt bad about yourself or uncomfortable and see how many of those are directly tied to something someone said to you, about you, or the way they said it.

One of the most powerful tools we have in our world is our language and the use of it with others. We can destroy someone's sense of self, destroy how they feel, incite anger and resentment, all with one word or phrase. On the other hand, we can also lift someone up, help them feel great, change their perspective of themselves the same way.

When we look at the original two areas these guidelines fall into, doing no harm to self or others and being aware of our intent, we can see how our speech has the regular power to not only do harm, but can also reflect poor intentions. We are so used to saying things that come to mind, we don't often consider if we should, or the best way to do so.

Things like gossip, creating false stories that make us look better, or creating embellished stories to make someone else look bad is so ingrained in how we were raised that it is hard to notice and overcome, but it is possible.

In our modern world we are inundated with opportunities to vent our frustration online through review sites, typically to bring someone down, or share an experience that didn't fit our view of how we thought it should be. These are used to share feelings, often times anonymously, so we can be even more caustic in our words. Few people spend the time to share good experiences, anonymity instead becomes an outlet to attack others with no chance of reprisal, or having to face that person in the process. This is presented in some way as an altruistic action to "help others" not share a bad experience, but instead has become a tool to vent anger and damage the reputations of others for no real cause. Our experiences one time may be different than the next, and we can easily succumb to our ego's disappointment for not getting what we wanted.

We also are ego driven most of the time in conversations, anxious to say what we want to say, without listening to the other person. We interrupt, we try to butt in, we talk over them, we raise our voices, so that we can be heard. Our opinion, our ego, trying to gain control of the experience or relationship. This is something we can work on and it becomes life changing in the process.

Focusing our attention to be more open by receptively listening to someone helps turn down our own inner monologue so we can hear, process and choose how to respond. The way we respond can now be more tempered, positive and supportive of that person. This is how we can positively engage with other people.

Opening yourself up to others around you also creates connections outside of your immediate world. My wife and I find ourselves in conversations with people who work in restaurants quite often. We listen to them when they share something, or we engage with them and ask about them. Not because we want something from them, because we really are interested in meeting people and engaging with them. I say "hello" to people I pass and smile. I respond when someone says something to me in the checkout line at the store. Many times people will look down, look away, pretend not to hear, fueled by the desire to not engage and stay in our own heads, and through this action we treat that other person like they are invisible and unworthy of our attention or response.

In my interactions with people at work, with people at our zen center, friends I see, I make a conscious effort to focus on them when they approach me. Engage in the connection and try to quiet my judgement, my inner voice, my ego. I wasn't always that good at this, especially in my past, and at times in my career. Stress levels that are so high that we become walking time bombs are a recipe for bad speech and communication. When we open our mouths a stream of anger and stress roll out. This has lasting effects on ourselves and others. Just as you have those memories of a time someone made you feel less than right, or invisible, or bad about yourself, you too have most likely done the same to others.

The key to all five of these personal guidelines is control of actions and intent. Watching how we move through the world and the effects we have on those around us takes dedication to maintain control of our choices. The framework provides structure, but we have to act within it, in the moment, to make better choices.

How you survive.

One area that is not directly covered by the five basic guidelines, but includes many of them, is how we survive or live in the world.

It is true that to live in our modern world we have basic needs and probably need to work to make enough money to survive in this time and place. We no longer hunt and gather for our meals, we don't only move locally from one walkable area back to our shelter in the mountain.

If you have to work to survive, as I do, we have to include these aspects of our choices in all places we go, not just when we are at the center on a meditation cushion. Living this lifestyle we are describing isn't something you do when you are off the clock, or on weekends when it's convenient.

I read a Gallop poll report that on average, adults who are employed full time in the US work 34-47 hours per week. That doesn't include the time we spend getting to work, eating lunch or driving home. Depending on your type of work, it could be much more. Many people in lower income brackets have to work multiple jobs to be able to survive, which adds to travel time and costs, without having those extra hours covered by pay.

The industry I have worked since I was young, is known for long hours at the office, long periods of time on a project, weeks and weeks of attention to getting something completed. Most times that included bringing that work home each night or on the weekends. I have since changed my work schedule so I don't live that lifestyle anymore. But I have also changed how I view my profession and the people in it to try and incorporate many of these aspects.

We spend so much of our days and weeks engaged in making money. We don't often stop and ask ourselves this question: "Am I doing harm through how I earn my income?" Or "Am I practicing what I believe in during my time at work with other people?" Or even the unheard of question in these times: "How much is enough, and do I need more?"
One of the ways we build a strong, disciplined structure in our lives is to not leave gaps in the fence. It applies to all aspects of our life, and how

we survive at the cost of others plays a role in this as well.

We are currently living in a time that is seeing large industries that make record profits while their employees can barely make ends meet. The heads of these organizations reap huge rewards on the labor of others, exponentially so over the last two decades.

People are so driven to make more and more money, they rarely stop to look at what it may do to others. It is the domination of ego, a "me first" mentality that goes far beyond just surviving in the world. Our humanity has gone from survival of the fittest to survival of the richest, and it is creating immeasurable harm and distress on people around them.

This is where we need to look at our involvement in our survival and what we can do to create a positive shift in the immediate environment around us and maybe even our broader society.

When my business partner and I started our company, we were aligned, thankfully, on how we treat the people we hire. We wanted to create an environment where everyone could first have a real work-life balance, where young people could be supported in such a way as to become the next positive leaders in our business, and where everyone shares in the rewards, both financially and personally.

In some ways, this means we make less than we could, but we have found a balance in that equation. We have created a business that can do all of those things, treating people like people, supporting them (because we actually care about them), guiding them and providing them freedom to live their lives.

For instance, we do not track their vacation days or sick days, like most companies. We want them to have time away to recharge. It allows them to be more happy and balanced, and when we provided that aspect, they are better at doing what they need to do at work. A rested happy mind is much, much more productive than someone after a 65-hour work week, putting long hours in behind a desk, or bringing work home over the weekend.

The corporate structure for large and small organizations has turned into hours for dollars, or how much can we get for our investment. It is even called "human resources," at most corporations which is a general term for the people who work there.

We instead look at our investment in growing and supporting great people as our return. Allowing them to be free, creative, productive and happy, is its own reward. And surprisingly, we all make enough to also survive and be happy in the process.

We may not always have a choice on where we work, and it would be naive to assume so. Not everyone can go create the perfect place to work. We took great risk in doing so, and managing it isn't always easy. Neither is our approach one that everyone would even want.
However, no matter where you work, you have an opportunity to be the person you want to be in regard to how you treat others, and what you

put into the world. If you are in a job you hate, working at a place you think puts bad things into the world, you may need to look elsewhere if you can. If you can't, then look at what you can do to change the outcomes in your job, or your role. How do you treat others on a daily basis? How do you respond to people you interact with? Are you watching your ego, motivations, intent and action? It only takes small changes within you to create a large impact on your environment.

I am reminded of a story I tell often as it relates to how we view the work before us.

My first experience in Japan, after a very long flight, was to go through customs, get our luggage and exchange money. When we arrived at the counter to fill out the form, there was an older man standing there in uniform, with white gloves, assisting people on filling out the forms to make sure they knew how to do it, to make sure it was correct and to help them get in the right line. His dedication to his job was extraordinary. He was focused, polite, enthusiastic and helpful. He treated his job, a job that would be considered a small menial job in the west, with the highest sense of professionalism and attention. Even in this job, that seems unnecessary, he was giving it his best, making it easier for people and creating a positive interaction for everyone around him.

If we can treat our experiences at work with the same focus, taking no small thing for granted, making a difference at every step, we would be better off as people and as a society. If that is impossible where you are, spend the time to find a place where you can. That may not be an easy choice, and I don't recommend you run out and just quit your job. But find something you can both survive doing and feel good about doing. Nobody gets to the end of their lives thrilled that they stayed in a job they hated for 40 years.

Building the bigger structure.

When I was a teenager, I was very upset about what I saw around me in the world. I saw, maybe too early to be able to handle it, how unfair and skewed the structure of our society was around me. It caused me great trouble, and caused me to develop a view of the world that I wanted no part of.

I however had a chance to speak with someone who told me this in a conversation: "If you are trying to defeat a structure, you just need to build a bigger one."

Now I took that differently at that time and I thought that meant something along the lines of "Build a bigger army to knock down your foes! Anarchy!!!" But over time, when that didn't necessarily work, I instead built a bigger structure within myself. A structure that allowed me to not knock down that giant one before me, but instead to walk around it and through it unopposed. I chose to walk a different way and build a life I thought would be worth living.

This is why we follow these guidelines and maintain the discipline needed to follow them. By building a framework around our thoughts and actions, we can get to the root of our intent behind those actions and start to really work at making ourselves happier people within our world, and make it better for those around us. No matter what situation we find ourselves in at this point, we can change and make a difference. You can start at any time, just start doing it and see what a difference it makes. It may not always go great, and you may not see results immediately, but we should at least start trying to make positive change where we can. It's not an easy task, but with the right tools, the right framework, and the right state of mind, you will accomplish some level of "better."

SECTION 4: MIND

For all of the things that go on in our lives, all the actions and reactions, all of the good times and the bad, our minds are at the center. The way we process and color each experience can be changed, gradually through the control of our thoughts, at the root of our intent, leading to better actions.

To be able to accomplish this, a strong mind is needed throughout our day. A strong mind, with good concentration, that can distinguish the difference between impulse and control, between the root of intent and our subsequent actions. It requires changes in your life to be able to have this clear, stronger mind.

This is not easy. It's good to know that going in.

It takes effort, from you, on a regular basis, over a long period of time to achieve this. As the saying goes "Rome wasn't built in a day." Although, lucky for us, it also won't take centuries.

This may be the hardest part for practitioners to understand and implement. The world will not change because you are good at meditation. It will also not cure you of stress, or make you a better person on its own. It won't get rid of what ails you. It will however provide a clear view on how you can make those changes yourself. With a clear view, we start to see the root of the problems, instead of trying to cover the symptoms.

I see this a lot in business, in the Zendo and in myself. We feel a symptom (like stress), and we look for the magic pill, or the practice, or the person to remove that stress for us. However, that stress is self created within ourselves due to something external, or something lingering internally that is manifesting itself in this way. It is a warning sign, just like the pain we feel when we touch something hot. Our body is reacting, sending our mind a message to stop doing that, it is dangerous to our survival.

By practicing meditation, we can feel better, more calm, more relaxed. So we think we have cured stress. But it doesn't last, because we just get stressed again as soon as we get off the mat, because we have yet to solve the problem. This is like drinking sour milk, feeling disgusted, getting the taste out of our mouth by drinking clear water, and then just going back to drink the sour milk again. It sounds ridiculous when it's described that way, but this is very often how we live our lives.

This was actually the problem that the Buddha ran into in his own training. Keep in mind, the man, Siddartha, when he left on his journey to find the answer to his own suffering, he didn't just walk out, sit down and wake up. It was after a long period of trying different forms of practice and working with teachers who taught meditation techniques. As he found out through this process as well, everything was great when he was meditating, but when he stopped, he was right back where he started.

Many years later, after he had established the sangha and was becoming well known, he wandered into a village. The head of the village approached him and asked why they should listen to him, as there had been many people at the time who came to the village with the answer to finding the end of suffering.

The Buddha simply said to not trust him at all, just because he said it, but to try it for themselves. Fully commit to it, not just a little, not just one part of it, or part-time, or as a hobby, or when they had time. Fully follow what he suggested and see if it worked. If it didn't, then find something else that did.

This is the problem we face, many of us, living in the modern world we find ourselves in. We want the benefit of living a better life, having more joy and ease and less suffering, but we want to do it once a week, for ten minutes and have all the benefit, without really any of the work.

This is the Western view of many things, and how we are raised to think. Do less, get more. Maximize our time for the most benefit and profit. Multitask our actions to maximum efficiency.

For all of the mathematical equations we can create to make our lives more efficient, and get more from less effort, the lifestyle we gain from this path comes down to this equation:

Find out what is causing your suffering
 + changing your life to stop those things
 = a changed life.

There are no shortcuts, there is no easier path and nobody can do it for you (including the Buddha). Only you can change, and only you are responsible to do so.

The effort required however is something gradual, more approachable, and more applicable than what most people would believe. If we, as the Buddha suggested, dive in, wholeheartedly, and try it with our very best effort, we see results. *The world may not change around us, but the world within us becomes something much different, and I think much better.*

When people ask me this question: "Why do you practice Buddhism?" I can answer confidently, "Because it works for me."

I studied for many years, read books, practiced meditation on my own (without much understanding of how to do it), but I didn't really see any change within me. However, when I started to actually work on myself, practiced with a sangha and teacher, regularly meditated with structure and purpose, I started to see the factors in my life that were causing my suffering. I saw the sour milk I was drinking over and over and found a way to remove it from my life.

Once that behavior was removed, I was able to remove other aspects, on and on. It is maybe also good to understand that balance in our lives, and the goal we are looking to achieve is not just a single upward direction.

The other side of the mountain.

Our lives are typically a series of peaks and valleys. For this reason it can feel like it is hard to find and sustain a balance. Sometimes, it can also be hard to tell whether or not we've even made any progress in the right direction, and this is why it becomes hard to feel like this concept of balance, or finding a center point, is possible since it seems to be contrary to how our lives really go.

When we start out on a new journey in life, we often use analogies such as "walking up the mountain," or "paths up the mountain." However, real life is much more like "summit-and-plummet." We climb many mountains along the way, and it can be hard, of course, when we hit the valley instead of the peak. It makes us feel like we've gotten nowhere, and instead ended up right back where we started. It's like our efforts have been wasted.

I like to ride rollercoasters, and this up and down, summit-and-plummet-styled journey may sound like a rollercoaster. After all, our emotional ups and downs often feel like we're stuck on one. But to be honest, I don't think a rollercoaster is an entirely accurate metaphor.

When you are on a rollercoaster, there is that anticipation as you slowly click, click, click your way to the top, but when you crest and go down the other side it's exhilarating and fun and wonderful and everyone is cheering, hands in the air.

I rarely see people go through life that way. They race to the top anyway they can, and when they go over the other side, the cheering stops.

When you get to the bottom on a roller coaster, the momentum brings us back up to what's next and anticipation begins again. In life we get to the bottom, and we think it is the end, we feel like that was the entire ride and we just want to get out of the car at that point.

There is a concept I learned from my time studying Taoism, called "The other side of the Mountain." It took me some time to fully grasp its significance. However, it is a useful way of thinking about our lives.

To understand the idea, first you need to bring to mind the image of a mountain that lies in front of you. From this vantage point you can clearly see the peak. Now, you don't really know what is on the other side of the mountain but you do know that after you reach the peak you will be going downhill. The other side of the mountain is terrain and territory we are unaware of because we have focused all of our attention on the climb up. We can look forward, we can see the peak, the summit as the goal, but after that goal, we go back down the other side, sometimes with great momentum.

Herein lies the problem. We are always focused on the build-up, getting to the top, when in reality all peaks require valleys, because by definition, without a valley there is no peak. A mountain without the other side is just a long uphill climb. We need the other side to define the mountain. What rises also falls, which is a natural aspect of the nature of the universe.

So these ups and downs seem inconvenient, but the valleys tend to be the most fruitful in our lives.

I have never met someone who said, "Life is going great right now, everything is in place, and I suddenly woke up and realized that I am creating my own suffering in my life and I am going to need to change." Nobody thinks that when all is well, everything is going great, and they're feeling wonderful. But after the peak is the other side of the mountain, and we are unprepared for that fall.

If I look back over my life (so far anyway), when something was hard, or when my situation changed, it was always the catalyst for something that was better on the other side.

There have been spiritual quests that turned out not to be what I thought, but instead led to a greater understanding of myself and brought me to "something that works" in my study and practice of Zen. There have also been obstacles in my career, health issues, money issues, and a whole host of challenges or "valleys." Almost every positive thing that happened in my life came from the other side of the mountain, not what I was aiming for. From hitting a peak, and moving past, down the other side and up to the next peak.

When we can accept the peaks and the valleys as part of the entire process, the goal of the climb, the acceptance and control of the descent, we can lean into it and gain momentum, so that when we hit that valley, we use it. The momentum we carry through the valley pushes us up the next peak a little easier, our struggle becomes easier and we don't stop in our tracks.

However, we typically throw on the handbrake when the coaster goes over the top and by the time we get to the bottom we have killed our momentum and we get stuck. This is why it can be so hard to climb back up the next time.

When we can view both sides of the mountain as one thing, one process of up and down in our lives, the top and bottom become less extreme, and we do reach a moderation — a balance between these states. We don't try and hold onto the top as much, because we know what comes next and we don't linger at the bottom, because we use it to push up to the next rise.

This is the balance we speak of, to keep the same focus on the way up, and on the way down. They become part of the same thing, not separated as the good times and the bad times. When our practice is consistent at both both points, no matter if you are at the top or the bottom, you are making progress along the way.

This takes effort, and concentration, and self-reflection, before ultimately we can see inevitable change in our lives.

Our mind creates our world.

The best way to start, is to start doing. This is not something you can think your way out of, you must have action to help change your thinking, and one of the best ways to start working on your concentration is through a regular, dedicated meditation practice.

Meditation's aim isn't to provide you a link to some spiritual plane of existence, it is a tool for you to use, like weights in a gym. It is a practice that allows you to watch your mind, see what arises, and train your concentration to be able to control the movements that lay within.

When we have introductory classes, my main intent is to start people off with something they can do on a regular basis, at home or with the sangha (but mostly at home), so it becomes part of their regular lifestyle.

This is an important distinction to make with starting a meditation practice, it is a lifestyle change, not a part time hobby. It should become as natural in your life as eating and brushing your teeth.

To start this practice you really don't need much. Just a place to sit comfortably.

It does help to have a dedicated place in our home where you can control some of the elements around you, like the lighting, the sounds, somewhere that doesn't have strong odors.

You can of course invest in a cushion and mat, but you can also use a blanket and pillow to get started.

Find a time that works in your life now. To start, ten minutes a day is all you need. Everyone can find ten minutes to sit. Find a point in your daily schedule that allows you to sit without distraction or the need to be somewhere immediately after. Many people sit in the morning, before they go to work, but you may need to make sure you allow extra time in your routine.

I have found one of the best times is just after work, before dinner, because at that point there is some flexibility on what I need to do next. You can also sit in the evening (instead of watching TV), or sit on your lunch break (if you have a quiet space to do so). It can be anywhere, any time that fits your life.

Once you find that time and place, commit to doing it on a regular basis. Tell people this time is for you and let them know you shouldn't be disturbed. Put it in your calendar if you need to, so you have a consistent reminder and you don't plan over that time.

If you are at home, and live with someone, or children, or pets, find a time you can be alone, or let them know this is important for you and they should respect that space and time for you. Again, this can't be something you do when you "have extra time" because you will never find it.

Time to sit down for a change.

Once you have established the time and place, sit comfortably. There is no "correct" way to sit as long as your posture follows these guidelines:

- Sit upright, back mostly straight, head up. This allows you to breathe regularly and avoid any fatigue on your back.
- If you sit on a mat and cushion, sit in the middle of the mat, so it supports your hips and alleviates pressure on your legs. Your legs can be crossed in front, but make sure you are not applying too much pressure if the legs touch. If you sit in a chair, sit on the edge of the chair, so you don't recline backwards.
- The hands can rest on the knees, or together in the center of your lap.
- Keep the eyes somewhat open, just slightly, so you can stay present and not fall asleep.
- Breathe naturally, no need to control your breath, but keep a normal pace.

Once you have gotten yourself in position, you are ready to start the ten minutes. You can use a timer if you wish (there are of course good digital applications for this). It is best to not stare at a clock. Ten minutes will feel like 1,000 minutes when you watch the clock, and you want to focus your mind elsewhere, so move any timer to the side, out of view.

If you wish to change your atmosphere, you can lower the lights, and burn a candle so your eyes can stay open without becoming fatigued. If the room has strong odor, burn some incense (mild tone incense, nothing too strong as it can become distracting). Make sure it is somewhat quiet. Natural sounds are ok, but if you live in a populated area, with loud sharp noises, you may want to wear headphones, or ear plugs. Sometimes when I find my area to be noisy, I may use a sound generating application that provides natural sounds or a repeating tone that allows me to have a background that isn't distracting.

As you begin to settle into meditation, your mind will become quiet due to the reduced stimuli. This is when you can see how active your mind really is.

Typically, when people start a practice, they are amazed at how the mind starts to conjure up all kinds of things in the space of silence. Stressors at work, problems we face, fears, what we have to do that day, what happened just prior to sitting down. It can be the constant stream of dialogue we carry around inside of us.

This is just the mind doing what the mind was developed to do, keeping you aware of your surroundings at all times. We tend to forget that we are a product of our ancestors that developed and survived because of this constant attention and awareness to dangers that lurked.

Now, our minds have shifted to be holders of all things, stimuli and ideas based on our lifestyles. Our minds control us constantly, feeding our desires, evoking various emotions and memories, drawing on our storehouse of preferences, and maintaining a running internal dialog in which we process conversations and create an imaginary interlocutor inside of us.

Single point of focus.

To be able to turn down the volume of our thoughts and feelings, we need to have a single point of focus. The practice is not to stop having thoughts (which is impossible), or to have no emotions (also not possible or even practical) or to completely shut off all external stimuli inputs (again, also impossible).

The practice is to find a single point of focus that allows those elements to find no traction. We bring our attention to a single point, one focus, and begin to allow those other elements to simply arise and pass on by. I liken this to using a computer, something most of us have done at some point in our lives. We may also have used a computer with a limited amount of memory, so it can only do certain things at the same time. You may have noticed that when you are running a program that takes up a lot of that memory, there isn't enough space in your computer to launch something else. This is because all of the other applications are competing for the same resources.

When we put all of our attention on our single focus, it is like using all of your computer's memory on one thing, and the other things find it hard or impossible to launch and run in the background.

This focus I am speaking of can be different for everyone, and you can have multiple points of focus to use in your practice, which helps to challenge you when your practice becomes stale. When you feel that focus is becoming too easy, and the mind can still run in the background, you can use something else to change your focus to and regain control.

This can be a mantra (a set phrase that you repeat). I prefer this method myself as it has worked best for me. There are many mantra people use in Buddhist practice, like "Gate, Gate, Paragate, Parasamgate, Bodhi Svaha!" (Gah-tay, gah-tay, pah-rah-gah-tay, pah-rah-sahm-gah-tay, bo-dee-svah-ha) from the Prajna Paramita Hridaya Sutra (known as the Heart Sutra).

It can be focusing on the name of Bodhisattva, it can be a whole sutra, anything that keeps your focus, which is key. If you create your own mantra and it is too simple, it is easy for all of those other thoughts to run the mantra over in your mind. Also, focusing on something that brings up strong emotions, or preferences, or memories can also make it harder. For instance, if you create a mantra like "I love hamburgers! I love hamburgers!" Over and over, what will probably happen is you will get hungry in a short time. Or if you use something like "I will overcome my challenges at work today!" You will eventually start to think about those challenges, about your co-workers, or about the tasks that lay in front of you.

I always recommend finding a mantra that is not easy to remember, so that the focus has to be strong in order for you to repeat it as you meditate.

You can also use a mala in your practice, a string of beads. This keeps you present, having the movement of your hands on the beads. You can move a bead each time you complete the mantra as a way to connect these two parts of practice, a physical attention and a mental attention, and it serves as a checks and balance, as you will know if your hand stops moving, or if you are just moving beads with no correlation to your mantra.

You can watch the breath, just breathing in and breathing out, but again it can be hard at the start to practice this way, because you may be distracted every easily, since we don't have to think about breathing.

Visualization can also help. Focus on a stone falling into a clear pond and watch the ripples move away and settle before another stone drops. If you are doing visualization, keeping the eyes closed may make it easier to concentrate.

When you begin your meditation practice, your mind and body will revolt, so be prepared. They are both used to being the center of your attention, and they will try and distract you, so stay focused, even if you feel pulled away from your practice. Over time this will become easier, and you will be able to reduce distractions more quickly.

Once you have completed the ten minutes, stretch your neck and back and arms for a bit. You can rub your hands together and then place the warm palms over your eyes. Once you stand and move on to what is next, try and sustain the calm mind you have created before you move immediately into something you have to do.

There is a concept used in martial arts that may be applicable for this post-meditation timeframe called Zanshin, or lingering mind. In martial arts, this means to have attention and continuation even after the technique is performed. In this case, we want to maintain the focus of the clear mind before we move to the next task or activity.

Ten minutes each day is a great way to start, or ten minutes four times a week until you can get to every day. Try and dedicate what you can in order to get started, and build from there.

As you continue to develop your practice, you can do so gradually by adding ten minutes at a second point in your day, or increase your sitting time to fifteen minutes, and eventually twenty minutes. It's best to add more time in meditation when you begin to feel that getting through ten minutes has become routine. Always challenging ourselves, like adding weights little by little in the gym, will allow us to grow stronger in our practice.

Walking meditation.

You may also want to try meditation in movement. Walking meditation is a great way to supplement your practice and get you out of your house, where it may be easier for you to be less distracted from your surroundings and other people.

In some ways, this practice is similar to seated meditation. We want to keep our head up, chin down slightly so we can breathe. Also, keep the hands either in the center of your belly (right around your navel), or folded together behind your back.

I would hope this goes without saying, but if you plan to try walking meditation, keep your eyes open. If you can find a path, or an area of a park that is easier to follow, it will make it easier. Be careful where you decide to walk, try and avoid the traffic or other dangers around you, as you want to keep your awareness focused just like seated meditation. You can still use a mantra in this process, and I often use my mala in my hands at my back.

The point of this movement is to stroll, nice and slow, mindfully moving from one foot to the other at a moderate and unhurried pace. Set a tempo that you feel you can roll forward, into one step, and followed by the next. Breathe regularly and try to avoid looking around too much.

Digging in our garden to find the root.

Self-reflection is also a large part of our practice and can also be integrated into your meditation.

Just after you complete your ten minutes (or longer), with a clear mind, look at what is coming up in your life or your thoughts. What are the things that cause you to be unhappy, or stressed, or uncomfortable. What do you drag out of your memory over and over to ruminate about.

I call this kind of reflection "getting to the root" in ourselves. To really understand what is going on in your life, you have to be a kind of archaeologist, you have to dig to uncover the truth.

While we refer to this as "self-reflection," I am often seeking a more accurate label. To really make changes in your life, you need to use self-MRI or self-CATSCAN or something like that, something that goes deep, deep enough to see past the surface of things and uncover the root of where our intent lives.

To get to the root of a flower, we may get distracted by the color of the petals and the scent. But if we are willing, we can follow below the flower, follow the stem, see the leaves that are gathering energy to feed the flower, and then go deeper still into the dirt and mud. When we push away the dirt we can see not only the main artery of the stem, but the roots that come from it branching like veins into the earth.

This is how we can look into ourselves and not only understand the depths of our self, but see all the branches that weave into other areas of our lives.

If it's not a flower we are following, but a weed, or something that we don't want in our life, we have to make sure we not only get the whole root, but all of the tendrils as well, carefully, so we don't destroy what is around it. There may be some parts of those weeds that are tied to flowers we hope to preserve and we need to take this slowly.

This process is very necessary and shouldn't be taken lightly. We can't dig through the self with a giant gas powered weed-whacker and just rip up everything. A weed-whacker can't distinguish between a weed and a flower. The good from the not-so good. It takes the focus and attention of a skilled gardener to know what to pull, and how to do so.

The roots I have grown.

For much of my adolescence and young adulthood I held a lot of anger and resentment towards things that happened in my past that didn't live up to my expectations. It wasn't always related to something someone did. Sometimes it was because of what they didn't do. Oftentimes I realized that my expectation of people and their responses or behavior never actually even took place. This created a lack of trust in others within myself, and created a root that grew and shaped how I acted around other people.

Now if I follow this weed in my life, (let's call it a weed since it wasn't really a flower), I can follow the branches and roots down the line and see how that affected not just my direct relationships, but many other aspects of my life. The tendrils that started to grow came from that main root.

In excavating my garden and examining my weeds and flowers I have been able to ask myself questions that allow me to distinguish what needs uprooting and what needs cultivating. Was this maybe why I shy away from close relationships? Maybe why I still have trouble talking to people sometimes or feel uncomfortable and introverted in those situations? Is this maybe why, even though I seem to enjoy engaging with people and teaching large groups of people, I am mentally and physically exhausted afterwards? Maybe this is why I have been self employed for much of my career and do not do well under other people's authority? Why I would rather do something myself than trust someone else to do it for me? This deeply embedded root of just this one part of myself, that was developed so long ago, has grown over time and has had an impact that I was not initially directly aware of, in many areas of my life.

When I became aware of it, I used to just cut off the top of the weed. Then a few years later it was in full bloom again. Snip again, cut it off, and yet again it grew. And like a lot of real weeds, it started to spread. So I started to fire up the weed-whacker and a lot of other things went out with those weeds into the garbage, some of them probably flowers.

But when I really spent the time, slowed down and found the right set of tools, I was able to move the dirt out of the way, and see all the roots, and then start removing them.

However, like I mentioned, each small tendril from the main root had become intertwined into the rest of my life, and pulling one out started to pull on a whole bed of tangled roots and weeds. So, even though it took a long, long time, I started to extract all of the little things and examine how they were intertwined. The feelings of being alone. The self-image issues. The problems with depression and sadness. The anger that was feeding the main weed (anger is strong manure for weeds). The need to be alone at times, away from others. The shyness, the anxiety, all of these things that came from my original weed of being disappointed in people at various stages in life. It created a whole field that I needed to dig up and replant. In some cases, I used tweezers, in others a shovel, but over time they were removed.

And now they can't grow anymore. They can't absorb as much energy which instead gets expended on the flowers and good things I want there. There are still traces, but they are no longer getting bigger, and I can adapt and change now, and in the future overcome them completely.

Unfortunately, like many of us, I have a lot of weeds, so my work is never really completely done. I have to be aware of new seeds that could take root and grow before I even know they are there. Some of those weeds and tendrils actually helped me to have the ability to overcome them, so not all of it is always bad, which is why we have to be careful in our practice. If I had not had these structures in my life, I may never have made it to the other side of that mountain and made progress.

So if you too find yourself stuck somehow with a weed, something that seems as though it keeps blooming over and over. Something in your life, your relationships, your worldview, you need to get out the small hand shovel and start clearing the base of these issues to really understand where they are coming from and how far deeply they have become rooted in your own garden.

To do this, you need to have a clear mind, quiet the noise from the past, turn down the anger and resentment or whatever you are feeling, just long enough to get to the root and slowly pull it away from the dirt.

If we can weed our minds on a regular basis, we start to have a lot of extra room to plant those flowers we have been missing. This clear mind and reflection will allow you to see where your life needs to change, where you need to alter your behavior, or where an influence in your life has become deeply rooted.

By doing this, one weed at a time, we can slowly start to change our lives and our minds to be happier, more balanced and not keep planting or fertilizing the weeds in our garden.

Be mindful of your mind's mindfulness.

When we can let go of the past, and stop worrying about the future, we can start to look at the single most important part of your life. This exact moment you are in.

This is the practice of mindfulness that comes from having a clear mind and your practice can also help you to make better decisions from moment to moment, as well as bigger changes in your life.

Many people teach mindfulness these days, as it has become a corporate buzz-word and shows up in many walks of life.

Unfortunately, now that the mindfulness craze has been around for a while, many people have not had the benefits promised by the advertising. This is because mindfulness just by itself, without the benefit of all the other elements discussed, is difficult to understand and hard to maintain. Anyone, after all, can be present to the here and now. We can have a very mindful person who, in the moment, chooses to do or say something that is not very pleasant or helpful. I am sure there are "mindful jerks" out in the world, who are very aware in the moment of what they are doing. Just being present is not a prescription for being a happier or better person, and in some cases can make things worse.

To understand what mindfulness is, we have to consider all of the other elements we previously discussed and then add this formula:

**The past + the present + the future
= current state of mind**

Our minds are developing new opinions based on everything we have done in the past, from preferences to experiences, memories and feelings. We also add into our present moment all of our wishes and hopes for what immediately comes next, what's to come this weekend, or when work is over, or when we retire, and so on and so on. We are also adding and processing and categorizing what our current situation is at the moment. Our experience of that moment is a combination of all these elements, smashing into themselves in our heads at any point during the day. This is what you most likely have running around your head when you meditate.

So we miss, through this mish-mash of past and future the only moment that is actually real, and that is the exact present moment you are in. The exact moment you are reading this, the exact moment you sit in meditation, the exact moment you speak to someone, or have an experience. We step right over it and then later treat it as past issues, or we create moments for our future that don't even exist yet.

Mindfulness is bringing all of the elements we have been covering to bear in each of these moments. The ability to understand how our minds work, what is arising and what our intent is at that exact moment.

The truth of the universe is that every moment is absolutely unique, and will never be the same way again. Energy moves, the universe moves, every living being moves, in some way, both big and small, and will not be repeated.

Which means even standing in a long line is totally unique and precious and should not be taken lightly. Being in traffic is totally unique and will never be exactly like it is in that moment. A rainy, cold, bad day when everything goes wrong, is as precious as a great day with perfect weather, with everything taking place just as you want it to.

This is the challenge with a mindful state, it seems great when you feel great. It's not great when you feel bad. So people who practice only mindfulness, devoid of any other aspect of the path miss the overlapping aspects of being mindful, such as the nature of the impermanence in all things, so each moment, whether good, bad, or neutral, is precious moment to moment. But we need to also recognize that each and every moment will arise and pass. No moment is permanent.

We also, through understanding how our mind works through concentration, create the suffering or joy in that precious moment. By seeing the truth of who we are and the world around us we can begin to see the larger picture of ourselves in that moment. Putting into practice the five guidelines we discussed earlier allows us to use that moment for compassion, or peace or joy and not create more trouble or suffering for ourselves.

Mindfulness in a vacuum, removed from the other elements we've addressed, isn't a good practice and can cause larger issues when we are experiencing suffering. It is a one spoke wheel, which we can understand won't roll very far.

However, when we bring all of our practice to bear, in that single moment, we build a series of mindful moments, each beautiful and unique, and little by little, we suffer less.

Even though we often search for what is next, or what comes in the future, we may hope that things will get better, or worry that things may get worse, we miss the only thing that is real at any moment. The exact moment you are in. It is the only point at any moment that matters.

Even though we talk about walking a path, we are often just looking at the path and standing still. We actually need to start moving towards a better way to live, make better decisions and have a clearer mind.

It may require you to do something drastic and just stop for a moment and take stock of your present situation and see what needs to change. Do the work, maybe make hard choices to be able to move forward again.

This is the life we have. It is conditional, limited and we have a choice to make. Remain in our suffering, stay right where we are, or start putting forth the effort needed to change, moment to moment.

SECTION 5: PUTTING IT BACK TOGETHER

Now that we have gone through the entire process of our minds, our lives, who and what we are and where we are going, we can progress to the next step. That step is deciding if you want to actually make positive changes in your life to be a better person, to feel better and to be happy.

This may sound like a funny question, but you may recall that I asked you very early on in this book: *Are you happy with the life you currently lead?* I can tell you that I had trouble answering that question when I first started out on this path myself.

It wasn't that I didn't want to be happy, more satisfied with the life I had, I just didn't know any different. I was comfortable in my dissatisfaction, it was what I knew. Trying to not be unhappy was actually an uncomfortable direction, because it caused me to face what was causing my unhappy state. That required changing things about myself and my life. That meant having to be a different person and that can be a terrifying proposition when you are warm and comfortable wrapped in your blanket of discomfort. Being miserable was the only way I knew how to be and it took real effort over a long period of time (which hasn't ended) to look within in order to change directions.

I can say it was worth it, if you are wondering this yourself right now. When people ask how or if this can actually help them, I can say I am currently living proof. It worked for me and continues to work for me and I don't plan to change my path because it continues to have an ongoing effect. Even when I stray from the path, even when I need a break (and we all may need a break from the work on ourselves) I still go back.

The results so far are much better then before I started. I want less, I am satisfied with less. I live a simplified life, I am way less stressed than I was. I sleep better, I feel better, I don't get angry as often or as long or over minor things. I can survive and actually enjoy what I do in the process. My mind is much more quiet, I can actually see what arises within me and, far more often than not, I can control my reactions much better, at least most of the time. Little by little I have been able to remove weeds from my past so they don't grow and choke out the flowers in my life. I can concentrate when I engage with people, I care about them much more than I ever did before. I can see the amazing life all around me and wonder about the grand nature of the universe I find myself within.

I changed.

The funny thing I never understood when I was miserable, but learned later, and maybe it will help you as well is that I was going to change anyway, it was inevitable. I just took control of the change and made it something that was a better version along the way. This has always been my choice and in my control, to live the life I wanted to live. I just didn't think it was. I looked outside of myself to blame the world for my suffering, but it was always a prison of my own making. *I made the bars and the lock and I even had the key in my pocket the whole time.* But all that time I still thought it was out there somewhere, that life I wanted, I just couldn't see past my jail cell.

So, now it is up to you to decide for yourself. You too have the power and ability to change your life. It is your life after all, you can choose how you want it to be and nobody can tell you otherwise, or do it for you. There is no easy way out, no express lane.

Just start walking.

The puzzle completed.

I removed all of the language and terms from the eightfold path in the previous sections, just so you may better understand these concepts without the barrier of having to make sense of foreign terminology, or having trouble with overly complex ideas (although some of it was kind of complex in any language).

Now, however, if you are interested in seeing what we actually just went through, I will add them back in. You can decide to just skip over this part if you want. Knowing the terms and the overlaying concepts won't help to understand them any further, but if you have looked at these before and didn't know how they all worked together, and are overlapping and connected, you may be interested.

At the very least, it may serve as a convenient general overview for reference later on:

The Middle Path: (**Majjhimāpaṭipadā**) covered in Section One. The ability to stay away from extreme views, thoughts or actions that are either too harsh or too soft, and to watch the effect we have on ourselves and those around us. Ultimately living to do no harm to ourselves and others.

The Eightfold Path:

Prajna: Wisdom, **Pranja Paramita** (the perfection of wisdom) covered in Section Two.

- **Great View:**
    - Understanding the **Four (Noble) Truths** (life comes with a conditional nature, we create our own suffering or dissatisfaction, this comes from attachment to outcomes and that we can through our own efforts change).
    - The Nature of the Universe is impermanent (**Anicca**) and all things change constantly and nothing stays in a permanent state, including us.
    - **Dependent Origination** (**Pratītyasamutpāda**), the truth that we are all completely connected at our root to all living beings in the universe.
    - We are a combination of the five **Skandhas** (**Rupa**, form and **Arupa**, mental formations) and nothing carries on when they are gone, save the energy that you are comprised of.
- **Great Intention: Ksanti Paramita** (forbearance and tolerance for all beings)
    - Our intentions are at the root of our actions and create ripples in the world around us that can affect ourselves and others

along the way. By watching our intent, we can change what we put into the world. This cause and effect starts with **Karma** (Intent) and creates **Phala/Vipaka** (result) that effects ourselves, those around us and the universe as a whole.

Sila: Discipline, **Sila Paramita** and the Five Basic Precepts (**Panca Sila**) covered in Section Three

- **Great Speech:**
  - Our words can be the vehicle that creates good or bad results, so we watch our speech as we watch the intent behind our speech in our interactions with those we encounter (and the voice inside our heads).
- **Great Action:** Including **Dana Paramita** (giving of our ourselves with no thought of return)
  - Our actions are also the result of our intentions, and the things we do can help or harm those around us. By watching our intent, we also cultivate better actions and create a better place for ourselves and others.
- **Great Livelihood:**
  - How we survive in the world provides us a chance to build a world where we can survive, but not at the cost of doing harm to others. Paying attention to our needs rather than our wants, we can make sure all people are taken care of while we also can have what we need to live.

Samadhi: Concentration, meditation, covered in Section Four

- **Great Effort: Viriya Paramita**
    - Staying on the path and working on ourselves can be difficult and uncomfortable and it takes a great effort to stay on the path to become better, happier people. We may even need to go through great changes in our lives to achieve that goal.

- **Great Concentration: Dhyana Paramita**
    - Meditation practice on an ongoing basis to quiet the noise in our heads and get to the root of why we think and act the way we do. Weeding the garden of our past anger and resentment so we can be more aware of our intent as it rises and be able to make better, more compassionate choices.

- **Great Mindfulness:**
    - Understanding that all forms, sensations, and consciousness converge and arise only in the present moment. Being able to know each moment is unique and precious and should not be wasted in the short span of life we have. Staying in the moment not tied to our past or our desires and unattached to an ego that wants everything around us to be a certain way.

ABOUT THE AUTHOR

Venerable Hoden (法田 / Bup Chon) was ordained as a Samanera (monk) at Seonam-sa Monastery in 2010 and as a Bhikkhu in 2016 through the Taego Order in Seoul, South Korea.

He currently acts as the Abbot for Dharma Gate Zen Center in Troy, Michigan, and as Vice-Bishop for the Taego Order American-European Parish, teaching a mix of Korean, Japanese and Western Zen

Hoden Sunim graduated Summa Cum Laude with a Bachelor of Fine Arts degree from Marygrove College in Detroit, and an Associates Degree in Buddhist Studies from Dong-Bang Seminary, South Korea. He has previously served as the Director of Education for the America-European Parish of the Taego Order, as well as an Associate Professor at the Institute of Buddhist Studies.

Made in the USA
Columbia, SC
04 September 2017